MEDIA, FEMINISM, CULTURAL STUDIES

Stepping Forward: Essays, Lectures and Interviews
by Wolfgang Iser

Wild Zones: Pornography, Art and Feminism
by Kelly Ives

Global Media Warning: Explorations of Radio, Television and the Press
by Oliver Whitehorne

Andrea Dworkin
by Jeremy Mark Robinson

Cixous, Irigaray, Kristeva: The Jouissance of French Feminism
by Kelly Ives

Sex in Art: Pornography and Pleasure in Painting and Sculpture
by Cassidy Hughes

The Erotic Object: Sexuality in Sculpture
From Prehistory to the Present Day
by Susan Quinnell

Women in Pop Music
by Helen Challis

Julia Kristeva: Art, Love, Melancholy, Philosophy, Semiotics
by Kelly Ives

Luce Irigaray: Lips, Kissing, and the Politics of Sexual Difference
by Kelly Ives

Helene Cixous I Love You: The Jouissance of Writing
by Kelly Ives

The Poetry of Cinema
by John Madden

The Sacred Cinema of Andrei Tarkovsky
by Jeremy Mark Robinson

Disney Business, Disney Films, Disney Lands
Daniel Cerruti

Feminism and Shakespeare
by B.D. Barnacle

D0920128

Detonation Britain

DETONATION BRITAIN

Nuclear War in the U.K.

Jeremy Mark Robinson

CRESCENT MOON

CRESCENT MOON PUBLISHING
P.O. Box 393
Maidstone
Kent, ME14 5XU
United Kingdom

First published 2001. Second edition 2008.
© Jeremy Mark Robinson 2001, 2008.

Printed and bound in Great Britain.
Set in Palatino 10 on 14pt.
Designed by Radiance Graphics.

British Library Cataloguing in Publication data

Detonation Britain: Nuclear War in the UK
1. Nuclear weapons – Great Britain 2. Great Britain – Military policy 3.
Great Britain – Politics and government – 20th century
I. Title

355.8'25119'0941

ISBN 1-86171-173-5
ISBN-13 978-1-86171-173-1

CONTENTS

	Preface	15
I	Megacide	17
II	Hell on Earth	47
III	America Goes Nuclear	71
IV	The Nuclear Club	83
V	Britain Goes to Nuclear War	101
VI	God and the Bomb	125
	Bibliography	139
	Illustrations	149

Preface

This book was published in the mid-1990s. Since then, much has changed – not least the events of September 11, 2001 and their aftermath, the 'war on terror', the war in Iraq, the war in Afghanistan, and many other conflicts. Much has developed in global politics, so that much of this book is out of date. Instead of rewriting the whole book, I have opted to republish as it was; it remains more a historical account of a particular time in world history, specifically the nuclear war powergaming between the superpowers in the Cold War and after, up to the middle of the Nineties, and the 'nuclear madness' that was at its height between the 1950s and 1980s. Some of the information in this book will be out of date – about budgets, arms deals, technologies, and nuclear policies. But there are still thousands of weapons ready to fire around the world.

So there are no references to more recent political developments, such in Iraq, Iran, Israel, Afghanistan, Korea, Live 8, or Osama bin Laden, or Saddam Hussein, or George W. Bush, or Tony Blair, or the political groups, such as anti-capitalists, who oppose some world governments.

But the paranoia and suspicion is still everywhere in contemporary society – even more so, perhaps. Or it's shifted into different areas. Now it's about terrorism, espionage, cells, and surveillance. Or perhaps it always was.

Jeremy Mark Robinson
2007

I

MEGACIDE

MEGACIDE

Megadeath does seem to be the norm for the 20th and 21st centuries, an 'atrocity exhibition' of our very own. The 20th century was a century of suicide, genocide – and 'megacide'. Since World War II there have been the acknowledged armed conflicts: the Korean War in the early 1950s, Vietnam (1957-75), the Arab-Israeli wars (1967, 1973, 1982), the Gulf War (1990-91), Bosnia (early/ mid 1990s) and on-going conflicts in Iraq and Afghanistan, among others. Apart from these well-known examples of armed violence there were around 150 wars and conflicts between 1945 and 1995. Between 1945 and 1977 there were eleven armed conflicts every day, on average. Since 1945 there have been over 2,500 nuclear detonations. About 7,200,000 soldiers have died in these conflicts. Adding civilian fatalities, the number reaches 33-40,000,000 (Ahlstrom, 1991). These figures do not take into account those who were maimed, made ill, raped, dislocated, impoverished or tortured. The figures for the wounded and the dead in the two World Wars are staggering: in the First World War, of 65,000,000 forces mobilized, 8,000,000 were killed, 21,000,000 were wounded with 6,600,000 civilians dead. In WW II, of 77-81,000,000 forces mobilized, 15,000,000 were killed, 25,000,000+ were wounded and between 26 and 34 million civilians were killed. Russia suffered by far the worst in World War Two: 7,500,000 military were killed, 14,012,000 were wounded, with between ten and fifteen million civilians killed.[1]

Of course, after every major armed conflict 'never again' is sworn by the great and the good. This usually means 'not in our lifetime'. That is, 'not this year anyway'. Because armed conflicts keep recurring. In the 'postwar' era, it seemed as if a major conflict, such as the dreaded 'Third World War', would never happen. People were too intelligent, too sensitive, too democratic to do it again. Yet the nuclear arms race and the Cold War has demonstrated – at a cost of billions of dollars – that many nations are not preparing for war, but are already well prepared for war. Indeed, they have the latest technology to help them win a conflict. In the 1980s some commentators claimed that nations were too interlinked economically to make war, and the 'military overstretch' or over-spending needed to be cut in order not to harm this inter-dependency.[2]

It is worth noting the sources of the figures in this discussion of nuclear arms conflict. Two of the main sources are the annual *SIPRI Yearbook*, published by the Stockholm Inter-national Peace Research Institute, and *The Military Balance*, published by the International Institute for Strategic Studies. Each source differs: not only *SIPRI* and *Military Balance*, but also the US government, NATO, the UK Ministry of Defence, the Russian government, and bodies such as CND and Bradford School of Peace Studies. Some of the estimates differ wildly, such as the number of jets that have nuclear capability in Europe: NATO says it had 170 (in 1983), but the *SIPRI Yearbook* reckoned on 2,073 with 2,859 more in reserve (Stephenson, 1983, 62). At this the Soviet Union said it had 464 aircraft in Europe with nuclear capability, but NATO said the figure should be 350. The *SIPRI Yearbook* estimated the Soviet Union actually had 2,460 aircraft, while *The Military Balance* reckoned on 3,075.

WEAPONS

The arms industry has its own poetry, a poetry of maximum devastation. The world, whether you like it or not, is full of extraordinary death machines. Listen: Soviet *Oscar* Class, cruise-missile submarines fitted with SS-NX-19 antiship missiles. American MX missiles (Minuteman MGM-118A *Peacekeeper*), 95-ton 3-stage solid-propellant missiles with inertial guidance using gyroscopes and accelerometers, CEP 150 metres, range: 8,100 miles, 21.6 metres tall, payload: a juicy 10 W-78 350 kiloton warheads, plus decoys. Then there's the 2,000-lb Electro-Optical Guided Bombs and the 3,000-lb Laser Guided Bombs of the early 1970s, a big improvement on the bomb technology of the 1,000-lb Walleye: the EOGB could be designated a target by a controller on a TV screen, then allowed to find its own way to the target. A-bombs, H-bombs and neutron bombs which'll go off all around the planet like fireworks. The fusion bomb mixes the isotopes H_2 and H_3 of hydrogen and generates the equivalent of 14 megatons of TNT. F-16s, Jaguars, Tornadoes, Mirages, F-4s, MiG 21s, Su-24s, *Blinder* and *Badger* jets. AGM-86B, SS-20, SSBS-S3, Polaris A-3, Minuteman III, SS-NX-17 missiles. And the missile launchers and tanks: Pershing 1A, Lance Honest John, M-110 howitzers, Frog 7, SS-C-

16.

The Russian Tupolev Tu-95 *Bear's* a huge long-range bomber, with a crew of six, a range of 7,800 miles, and a hefty payload of 25,000 lbs; the Tupolev Tu-22 *Blinder*, with a maximum speed of 1,400 miles, has a payload of 20,000 lb of bombs. The Tupolev Tu-16 *Badger* can carry up to 19,800 lbs of bomb up to a range of 3,560 miles. The Tu-26 *Backfire's* top speed is mach 2.2, with a range of 5,530 miles carrying 22,046lbs of bombs. It can carry out conventional or nuclear attacks, anti-ship strikes, reconnaissance and low-altitude flight. The *Backfire* is the Russian bomber most likely to be used against British targets. In 1989 Russia was producing 30 *Backfires* per year.

The Su-24 *Fencer* has a weapons expert beside the pilot to operate the electronic navigation system which enables the jet to fly at low levels at night or in bad weather. The Su-24 might be escorted by MIG-23 *Floggers* or the long range MIG-25 *Foxbat*. The MIG-27 fighter-bomber carries conventional bombs, electro-optically guided missiles and AS-9 passive homing anti-radar missiles.

The NATO-codenamed Russian *Blackjack* is similar to the American Rockwell B-1B bomber, carrying air-launched cruise missiles or freefall bombs up to an amazing 9,075 miles without refuelling, to speeds of mach 2.3. Other Russian aerial hardware includes the MIG-25 *Foxbat* B and D, the MIG-21 *Fishbed* H, and the An-12. The phallic look and intention of military weaponry is obvious to many commentators. Joan Smith wonders why manufacturers give weapons such boring names (such as the ANX-13). Why not speak of 'Phallic missiles targeting Baghdad' and 'Macho-man missile launchers'.[3]

And don't forget the lovely nuclear submarines, bristling with warheads: *Delta*-Class, *Yankee*-Class, *Lafayette*-Class, *each sub-marine delivering more explosive than all that dropped in the Second World War*. The USA's first nuke-powered submarine,

Nautilus (1955), was more revolutionary than the dreadnought and the iron-clad ships of earlier years in the century. It could stay submerged indefinitely by recirculating air through carbon dioxide scrubbers; it could dive to over 1,000 feet and travel at over 20 knots; at these depths, the *Nautilus* could evade sonar and was fast enough to evade most enemies. When the Polaris solid fuel ballistic missile was developed, the nuclear submarine became a formidable weapon, for the submarine-launched ballistic missile was very difficult to detect. In 1983 The American Poseidon C3 missiles was carried on 19 *Lafayette*-class subs, each sub had 16 missiles, with between six and fourteen 50 kiloton MIRVed warheads on each missile. In 1983 Trident C4 missiles were carried by 13 submarines (12 *Lafayette-class* subs and one *Ohio*-class sub). Trident D5 was carried on two subs in 1983 (USS *Ohio* and USS *Michigan*), which were twice as big as the *Lafayette*-class submarines. The MIRVed Trident D5 warhead carried between 14 and 17 x 150 kilotons. Britain's submarine force in the mid-1980s consisted of 4 R-class sub (*Resolution, Renown, Revenge* and *Repulse*) which each carried sixteen missiles: these had 3 200-kiloton MARVed (not MIRVed) warheads on them. The Chevaline programme updated the A-3 Polaris missile with 6 50-kiloton MIRVed warheads. The new Trident D5 programme of the mid-1990s aimed (in 1983) to have 4 Trident submarines with 16 missiles a piece, each equipped with 8 MIRVed warheads.

But this is not all our guardians are doing for us, because right now the atmosphere, the very air we breathe, is buzzing with commands, counter-commands, decisions, arguments, prayers, from every radar base, jet, ship, satellite, submarine and Command Centre. Computerized commands and codes fly even now from military centres to Pershing II missiles – W84, SSM, airburst, 40-kiloton yield – and out of the window maybe soon you'll see the flights of Tu-95 *Bear* jets coming in for another dropload, and hear the scream of towns burning after a W78 Minuteman III ICBM 330-kiloton yield attack. You'll hear this and other floccinaucinihilipilifications.

For, terrifying though it is to contemplate, there are people – usually (white) men in suits and anoraks, it must be said – who dream of LGM-30G Minuteman III missiles, with their Triple MIRV warhead with penaids, Mark 12A with 335-kiloton thermonuclear warheads, length: 18.2 metres, speed at burnt-out: 15,000 mph, range: 7,000 kilometres. Minuteman III missiles, with Mark 12A warheads, 375 kiloton yield, with an 88.4% chance of killing a silo or military installation hardened to withstand 1,000 psi over atmospheric pressure. A nice thing to do in an attack is to target chemical stores: breaching a 50-tonne chlorine store, for example, will yield a 50% death rate up to around 1.4 kilometres from the store.

And there are people who muse about – and design and construct and control – MSBS M-4 missiles, 150-kiloton yield, which are ready for impact. Their primary targets are, among many others: Bristol, Singapore, Buenos Aires, Melbourne, Teheran, Tripoli, St Petersburg, Tashkent, Lisbon, Dakar, Dallas and Mexico City.

The superpowers once armed themselves with (and still retain) Su-24 jets, MIG-23 *Floggers*, long range MIG-25 *Foxbats*, MIG-21 *Fishbed* Hs, An-12s and MIG-27s, all armed to the teeth. The British Avro 4-engine Vulcan of the 1950s was planned to fly at 65,000 feet, 645 mph, to its target with its payload of atomic bombs. We live in a world of B-52H strategic bombers, range 16,000 km, payload 70,000 pounds, and SS-N-18 Mode 3 submarine-launched ballistic missiles, 7 MIRV, range 6,500 km, total yield over 150 megatons. Just 150 megatons, not much, really, just enough for breakfast, just enough to make sure you don't walk again, not after the ground burst or air burst, in the attacks on New York, Washington, Seoul, Lima, Caracas, Delhi, Jerusalem, Cairo, Johannesburg, Santiago, Los Angeles, Chicago, Paris,

Berlin, Mombasa, Bombay, Calcutta, Baghdad, Sydney, Hong Kong, Bangkok, Montreal, Oslo, Moscow, Toronto and Prague.

These are just some of the sites that will be targets. But don't worry, your town won't be left out. They'll make sure everyone gets invited to the Party. They'll make sure you get your fair share of megatons. You're on the guest list. You live on planet Earth so you must be invited, don't worry. Everyone is MAD, that is, they are assured of Mutual Assured Destruction. 'Those who devise nuclear strategies and talk of megadeaths are already insane.'[4]

Wait a minute, there's more: the F-117 'stealth' bomber can drop just one bomb and do what it took B-17 bombers on 4,500 sorties to do, dropping 9,000 bombs, in the Second World War.[5] In Vietnam this would have required 95 sorties and 190 bombs. The B-52 bombers in Vietnam carried 15 tons of explosives, but were vulnerable to Russian SAMs and could not fly near centres of population that were politically sensitive. Another example: it took 800 sorties in the Vietnam War to try to hit the Thanh Hoa bridge. Despite losing 10 planes, they still couldn't do it. Four F-4 jets later destroyed the bridge in a single pass (using early versions of 'smart' bombs).

It's not all sexy hardware and gadgets, either, in the arms race. There is years of training. The US Army TRADOC (Training and Doctrine Command) is the largest educational system in the Non-Communist world. TRADOC helped with the development of J-STARS (air-based radar system), MLRS (multiple launch rocket system), ATACMS (missile system), M-1 Abrams tank, Patriot missile, Apache helicopter and the Bradley battle vehicle. The AWACS and J-STARS were very successful in the Gulf War. The AWACS Boeing 707s scanned the sky in every direction, producing targeting data and detecting enemy missiles and aircraft. The J-STARS (Joint Surveillance and Target Attack Radar System) delivered accurate pictures of enemy movements from as far away as 155 miles, in all weathers. Two J-STARS aircraft flew on 49 sorties, identifying tanks, trucks, convoys, personnel carriers and artillery – more than 1,000 targets. The J-STARS controlled 750 fighter jets, with a success rate of 90% of finding the target on the first pass.

A Rockwell Tactical Systems Division advert in *Jane's Defence Weekly*:

> Affordable Advanced Weapons Technology. It takes both accuracy and affordability to deliver a truly efficient weapons system. That's why the perfect choice is the Rockwell GBU-15/AGM-130 family of standoff weapons.[6]

Who is the audience for this advert? Who reads *Jane's Defence Weekly*? Do major governments read it, wondering what weapons system to buy, much as people leaf through holiday brochures or the DIY section of the Sunday newspapers? While some people are wondering which fitted kitchen or conservatory to buy, other people are seriously considering the best way of blowing the enemy up

Another advert in *Jane's Defence Weekly* reads:

> Rosvoorouzhenie: State Corporation for Export and Import of Armament and Military Equipment. Total solutions you can rely on. "Rosvoorouzhenie" means not only "Russian Armament" but first of all total solutions to your needs. Representing the dynamic potential of the Russian defence industries, as the state arms supplier we have been operating for 40 years in the world's arms markets.[7]

The jargon of the defence package on the radio is bemusing: C3, SAC, DCS, BMEWS, COCNAADC, Green Pine and Giant Talk radio networks. The Soviets had (still have) gigantic radar ships – big liners and cruisers fitted with enormous spheres and dishes as wide as the ships themselves. The American C3 and C3I (command, control, communication and intelligence) system pivots around satellites (surveillance, warning, communications and meteorology), undersea and ground warning systems, global datalink networks, automatic data processing equipment, global voice, telephone and computer links, and land, sea and air command posts.

DEW, AWACS, NORAD, ASM, CEP, TEL, TNF – the global machine lumbers along, despite recent political developments (such as late 80s arms 'reduction' or the fall of the Berlin Wall). Proliferation, arms control, NATO, G7, arms embargo, you might not know what it all means, but you'll feel it when it hits you.

Large FAE (fuel-air explosive) bombs weighing 45 kilograms could have the same blast effect as the 'blockbuster' of WW 2. The CBU-55 bomb is nice. It contains three 33 kg 'bomblets' which release clouds of ethylene oxide vapour which extend 50 ft in diameter by eight ft deep. After 150 milliseconds the cloud is detonated by a delay action igniter. The explosion's 5 times more powerful than the same weight in TNT.

And there are people who dream of the Vought Corporation's Miniature Homing Vehicle – a cylinder or 'hittile' 12 inches in diameter, 13 inches long, which is ejected from an McDonnell Douglas F-15 Eagle fighter at the top of a zoom climb at a speed of 17,5000 mph. Sensors home in on the target. The onboard computer guides the cylinder to its target using mini-rockets. It destroys the target not with explosives but by simply smashing into it at 17,500 mph. It is the sheer speed and force which destroys the target, just pure brute force, slamming into a target at 17,500 miles per hour. The third stage of the Vought ASAT missile hits the target at 30,680 mph. How luscious. It's the ultimate in violence, penetrating the love object at 17,500 miles per hour.

There are people who control the military satellites, locked in their geostationary orbits like technological guardian angels, whispering to command centres about secret manœuvres, with their atomic clocks that lose only one second in 30,000 years. The technology for space surveillance is improving all the time: The Russian Nomad system, with its resolution down to around 5 metres, is commercially available. This means that many governments worldwide will be able to possess the technology to produce imagery of targets to within an accuracy of around 15 feet (Toffler, 244).

There is also an information and espionage war, being fought not with weapons but with computers, spy satellites and electronic espionage. The 1980s and 1990s were an era when terms such as cyberspace, hyperspace, information superhighway, internet, Worldwide Web and virtual reality were in common usage. In the 'infowar' of computers and cyberspace, 150,000 military computers were linked via the Internet.[8] The vast amount of data in computers meant that they were/ are prime targets for an enemy. Even more 'unreal' were the accounts of 'psychic espionage', in which psychics were used, for example, as 'remote viewers', to visualize buildings in which hostages were held.[9] This is the more bizarre (perhaps preposterous) end of military and intelligence systems.

The world may be on Panic Alert, Attack Warning Red, and we mightn't know. We've been close to ignition many times, it seems. The atomic clock is set at two minutes to midnight, scientists say. In other words: catastrophe is imminent.

There were/ are forty thousand megatons ready to go. Or is it seventy thousand megatons?

The new 'smart' or 'intelligent' weaponry, which was developed from the 1960s onwards, has altered military policies and war strategies. There were, for example, 'non-lethal' weapons, developed in the 1980s, which rendered enemy installations defunct but did not kill personnel. This kind of 'non-lethal' tactic was applauded by some factions of the military, but not by others. It wasn't macho to leave the enemy still standing: the age-old policy of the most ancient form of war (kill the enemy) prevailed, despite the new technology making human death unnecessary.

Killing or maiming by sound is another nice option. What you do (as France and other countries have done) is use advanced infrasound generators on say, a crowd, in order to control them. As the machines send out very low frequency sounds, the potentially naughty crowd vomits, defecates and becomes generally confused. It's one way of controlling an unruly crowd. Low frequency sound might also make sieges such as the Waco and Temple Mount (Jerusalem) less harmful. Laser rifles are a tasty possibility. They sound like science fiction, but have been tested already: they can flash-blind people, and do permanent damage. There are thousands of laser rifles around the globe. They were used by Soviet forces in Afghanistan. The Alpha chemical laser, developed by the US Defense Department, can produce one million watts of power, in order to hit an oncoming enemy missile.

Ecological warfare is also a possibility. It's had a long history: the Romans salted the fields around Carthage, while Russian soldiers had the 'scorched earth' policy in the Second World War. In Vietnam 300,000 acres of crops were sprayed, and 8 million acres were defoliated. Ecological warfare includes ruining crops with insects that have been modified genetically; changing the weather over the enemy's territory; or blasting a hole in the ozone layer with a laser; causing earthquakes or volcanoes with an electromagnetic pulse; altering winds. Other ways of fucking things up for your enemy include: 'liquid metal embrittlement' (spraying a liquid onto metal – bridges, weapons, airports – so they turn brittle and breakable); spraying lubricants on runways, stairs, railways, to make them unusable; or gluing things down (polymer adhesives can glue equipment down); contaminating fuel supplies or altering fuel to ruin engines.

'Smart' technology was the buzzword of the post-Gulf War military culture. At the carefully-scripted press conferences during the Gulf War[10] the media was shown video replays of bomb attacks where the missile would loop three times around the building, enter through a toilet window, navigate a maze of corridors, and eventually knock out a computer terminal. Or so it seemed. The 'smart' technology seemed to be a dream technology, capable of performing astonishing military tasks. The *Nighthawk* 'stealth' bombers (F-117s) accounted for forty per cent of the attacks on strategic targets, even though they flew only 2% of the total number of sorties. More than 3,000 computers in the Gulf War zone were linked to computers in North America.

In the 1990s the US Army investigated 'smart' armour for tanks: a web of sensors measures an approaching missile, sends the data to the tank's computer, which fires explosive tiles on the tank's exterior in order to deflect the projectile. The ideal 'smart' mine, too, is one that does not simply wait for the enemy to drive over them: it scans the enemy's vehicle, identifies its type and size, and fires a suitable explosive at it. If you are in a tank, though, you'll probably be attacked by a neutron bomb. The fast neutrons pass through any type of armour, at ranges up to ten times the blast and heat radius.

Robots – unmanned military vehicles – can perform a host of duties in a war scenario. They can carry out bomb defusing, repair equipment, patrolling, surveillance, planting sensors, clearing away mines, repairing runways, destroying enemy radar, and so on. No less than 57 different tasks can be carried out by military robots according to a spokesman of PHD Technologies Inc.[11] The Defense Advanced Research Project Agency in the Pentagon was researching robot vehicles from the early 1980s. The SHARC project investigated how groups of robots might perform military tasks. With robot technology, human lives are not put at risk: plus it's cheaper to have one computer operator controlling six tanks instead of having them full of 'soft skin' soldiers.

Soldiers themselves are valued highly by military strategists.

They have to know about geometry, topography, navigation, artillery, mortars, armour, mines, counter-mine weapons, engines, laser designators, thermal sights, satellite communications, radio, ammunition, demolition, the logistics of supplies and transport, and so on.

Parachutists with FXC Guardian parachutes can be dropped from 35,000 feet, 25 miles from the target, and parasail to it, reading a map, identifying other soldiers with infrared devices, landing into a 10 metre zone. Soldiers have to be protected: the 1980s saw a rise in 'Exo-Skeleton' or 'Exo-Man' technology, the SIPE (Soldier Integrated Protective Ensemble'), an all-over suit that protected the soldier against chemical, biological and nuclear devices. The 'Exo-Skeleton' came equipped with night-sight goggles and a heads-up display; there was a targeting system that tracked the eye's movements and pointed the rifle wherever the soldier was looking. Tiny robots, or 'nano-robots', were also developed in the 1980s and 1990s: nano-robots were small enough to navigate human bloodstreams. They were self-reproducing machines which could be activated at a given signal after lying dormant for 10 years.

Britain's intelligence services include the Secret Intelligence Service (MI6) and the Security Service (MI5); related bodies include the Overseas Economic Intelligence Committee, the Official Committee on Security and the Co-ordinator of Intelligence and Security. The Security Service (MI5) has operations dealing with Intelligence Resources and Operations ('A', directorate), counter-espionage ('K'), and 'domestic subversion' ('F', such as, in the 1980s, infiltrating the left wing and trade unions). In leafy, Regency Cheltenham is the Government Communications Headquarters (GCHQ) which is a huge electronic eavesdropping service. In the mid-1980s GCHQ employed 20,000 staff in 20 divisions, maintained by a budget that was rumoured to be four times that of the combined amount allocated to MI5 and MI6. Top projects for GCHQ included 'J', signals intelligence from the Soviet bloc, 'H', code-breaking, and 'X', computer back-up.

Electromagnetic pulse warfare is juicy. You detonate an electromagnetic pulse warhead in the skies over some electron-ically-sensitive area (a communications or financial centre) and it damages the electronic systems (such as Quotron machines, data transmission lines, stock and bound markets, commodity trading systems, bank transfer networks, credit card networks). An electromagnetic pulse warhead exploding over the financial centres of Tokyo, Frankfurt, London or New York would create chaos in the economic world. In the age of the 'info-terrorist', computers can be hacked into and damaged. In the mid-1990s there were over 100 million computers in the world, millions of them linked together. There are rich pickings for an 'info-terrorist'. In 1988 one electronic finance transfer network in the US (Fedwire) handled 235 trillion dollars in money transfers. 'Viral predators' or 'crackers' can infiltrate computer networks and do more damage with a computer keyboard than with a conventional bomb.[12] Hi-tech computer espionage and hacking means that millions of top secret files can (potentially) be intercepted. 6.3 million documents of a 'classified' nature were churned out by the American administration in 1992, some of which could be easily hijacked; others might be more difficult.[13]

Space warfare became increasingly important in the 1970s and 80s. The SDI ('Stars Wars') programme was only the more publicly acknowledged ingredient in a widespread investment in military space technology. In 1987, for example, there were 850 launches of space hardware and missiles. Russia and America launched 700 of these: by 1989, though, the number of launches was 1,700, 1,000 being those of nations other than Russia or America. A raft of new missile technology was developed in the

1980s by the non-superpower nations: India tested the Agni missile in 1989 (range: 2,500 miles, warhead: 2,000 pounds), India also had a tactical missile in the early 90s, the PRITHVI; nations such as Libya, Syria and Yemen had the Frog-7 missile (range: 70 miles, warhead: 1,000 pounds).

Reagan's SDI programme was from the first lampooned. In 1991, George Bush streamlined (called down) the programme; by 13 May 1993, President Clinton called an end to the Strategic Defense Initiative. Even so, space is now filled with all manner of junk, much of it military (three-quarters of satellites have a military link). There are, in fact, three and a half million bits of junk in orbit around the Earth, from flecks of paint to old rocket boosters. The weight of this junk is over 2,000 tons. The plans for the colonization of space are impressive, but keep getting put back (due to funds and politics). Space nuts want us to leap out into the colonization of the Solar System and space as soon as possible. Politicians and company directors are more cautious.

The space station Alpha was supposed to start being built in orbit in 1996, but was cut back. 31 launches would be required to fit together the American Alpha station with the Russian Mir 2 station: this was intended for the late 1990s. Plans were developed for a post-Shuttle craft, that could get into space and back much cheaper. Boeing claimed their two-stage-to-orbit craft would be operational by 2002. The British-Russian HOTOL craft would be lifted to 6 miles by a Russian Antonov 225 and then use rockets to propel itself into orbit. The American X-30 or American National Aerospace Plane, was to use supersonic ramjets to achieve an orbital speed of Mach 25. Another idea was the tether and elevator, to carry up items from Earth to space stations. Then there's the moonbase notion: in the early 1990s NASA projected four people on the moon, staying for about two weeks. By 2010 a crew of twelve could be based on the moon for up to a year. The initial tasks on the moon might be 'scientific': a radio telescope, geological surveys, but industrial uses would soon become necessary to support the massive cost. Mining of the moon's minerals and resources is inevitable.

Then there's Mars, another long-cherished sci-fi goal. The *Mars Together* project would involve the Russian Mars rover *Marsokhod* which would travel perhaps hundreds of miles of the surface of Mars over two years; a huge helium balloon would drift above Mars, mapping and taking pictures. A manned Mars mission would (in early 1990s prices) cost between $50 and $500 billion. Six astronauts would spend 500 days on the planet, and the journey time would be 120-180 days each way (if a nuclear rocket was used). Asteroids are rich in minerals, including gold. The asteroid 1986 DA is estimated to have 100,000 tonnes of gold and platinum, 10 billion tonnes of iron and 1 billion tonnes of nickel. One idea is to mine the asteroids by dragging them closer to Earth by planting a mass driver on them: this is an electrical solar device that uses power from solar panels to accelerate material mined the from asteroid down a pipe. As the material is ejected through the pipe, it powers the asteroid towards Earth.

The biggest problem about space is the sheer size of it, meaning lengthy voyages, i.e., costly projects. Crossing the vast distances of space must be cheap as well as quick. For example, the nearest stars are in Alpha Centauri. It would take a rocket 50,000 years to reach the nearest stars of Alpha Centauri (4.3 light years away, or about 43,000,000,000,000 km). Thermal-nuclear rockets may be used for Mars missions. Cargo spaceships may be powered by electricity: an array of solar panels or a nuclear reactor will make electricity and create a strong electrical field. Ions from an inert substance (such as xenon) will be accelerated into a high speed jet. Sailing across the Solar System is another sci-fi-style notion: giant sails or kites 1 km across will use a wind of sunlight to power them (albeit slowly at first). The British Interplanetary Society's *Daedalus* project is an unmanned spaceship driven by little fusion explosions. Small amounts of helium 3 would be ignited by an electron beam, 250 times a second. After four years the spaceship could reach a speed of 4,000 km per second, or one-eighth of light speed. The nearest planetary system outside the Solar System may be around the star Tau Ceti, around twelve light years away. Or around Epsilon Eridani, a star younger and smaller than the sun. Barnard's Star is relatively close (6 light years) but is cool and old, and is probably orbited by dead planets. To reach even the nearest planetary systems, then, spaceships will have to travel at near-light speeds. Using anti-matter is another option out of *Star Trek*. The trouble is, making anti-matter is expensive, let alone difficult to store. At mid-1990s prices, anti-matter would cost $8 billion to produce just one milligram. A journey there and back at 1/5 of the speed of light would require 5,000 tonnes of fuel.

All of these space age projects sound fabulous – they are in the true spirit of voyages of discovery and bravery. It is the frontier spirit that is declared at the beginning of every *Star Trek* episode: 'to explore strange new worlds'. It was this spirit that (partly) powered the euphoric, idealistic age of the Moonshots of the late 1960s and early 1970s. In the post-Cold War, ever more cynical era, space exploration must always be economically and politically sound. Plus, as is obvious, but needs stating, there will always be a politico-military dimension to space exploration. After all, if three-quarters of the objects in space so far (satellites in orbit around Earth) have a military function or link, then one can expect that a large proportion of anything happening in space, in or out of the Solar System, will be military.

MONEY

The arms industry costs 1,000,000 dollars per minute (1982 figures). That's $16,500 per second (compare this with the amount in the title of Raymond Fletcher's 1963 book *60 Pounds a Second on Defence*). 100,000,000 people worked in the military forces worldwide or in back-up services in 1982, and arms are second only to oil as a money-making enterprise. It's worth remembering, too, that while the West spent about 5% of its income on arms (in 1983), the Warsaw Pact countries was spending 11-12%. The US spent around 30% of all private and public research-and-development funds on military schemes. In 1979 the military budget of the world was $478 million. The world's armed forces were 24.46 million.

It is not the warheads but the delivery systems that are expensive. In 1983 one F-14 jet cost $22 million; a B-1 bomber cost $102 million; a British guided-missile destroyer cost $195 million; a main battle tank was $1.5 million; a torpedo was $1.1 million. In 1983 bombers were costing 200 times what they did in the Second World War; fighters cost 100 times more and aircraft-carriers 20 times more (Wilson, 1983, 177). Comparative costs reveal that one fighter could inoculate 3 million children at $3 each; one torpedo would provide permanent clean drinking water for 150,00 people; one nuclear submarine and its missiles could buy 100,000 working years of nursing for the elderly. Nuclear arms are expensive in another way: they are not good value for money, because they can never be used – not on a large scale. They are an enormous insurance policy.

The chief military contracts in America in 1982 were, among others: General Dynamics ($5,891,000,000), McDonnell Douglas ($5,530,000,000), United Technologies ($4,208 million), General Electric ($3,654 million), Lockheed ($3,498 million), Boeing ($3,238 million), and companies such as Rockwell, Grumman,

Northrop, Westinghouse, Honeywell, IBM, RCA and Ford (in the mid-1990s, British Aerospace was fourth in the league table of defence companies).[14]

The US defence industry was/ is concentrated in a few cities, not spread over the whole US (General Electric in Boston; United Technologies in Connecticut; McDonnell Douglas in St Louis; Grumman in Long Island; Boeing in Seattle; Lockheed, Northrop and Hughes in LA; and General Dynamics in Dallas and Fort Worth). The big companies have large R & D departments (research and development) which develop laudable technological space-age projects while also pursuing military projects. In the early 1980s Lockheed developed NASA's space shuttle and telescope but also Trident I and II missiles and cruise missile carriers. The development of public-spirited, feel-good projects such as NASA and space age technology by the big aerospace companies enables them to pursue the real money-making projects (i.e., military-related) away from the public eye. It was research into the US space shuttle that helped the development of the 'space bus' delivery warhead launch system. The MIRV (multiple independently targeted re-entry vehicle) system was developed by the main contractors of the space programme (Lockheed, Lincoln Laboratories, Aerospace Corporation and RAND).

For the big US aerospace companies, the Department of Defense contracts guarantee a huge income over many years, and account for over half their income. In 1975-79, General Dynamics gained 67% of its income, with $3.52 billion; McDonnell Douglas gained 63% with $3.25 billion; Fairchild Industries had 87% with $559 million; Northrop had 63% with $1.22 billion; and Grumman gained 85% with $1.32 billion. Even when the US aerospace and military companies use independent investment for their research and development, the Department of Defense still reimburses them. In the case of Grumman, for example, 78% of their $237.7 million independent R and D investment was reimbursed by the

Dept of Defense. Northrop had 50% of its $173.1 million investment reimbursed. For multi-national US companies like Lockheed, 88% of its aerospace business stems from military contracts. As one commentator put it, '[i]n both America and Great Britain, the aerospace industry is effectively a war producer.' (Prins, 1983, 150)

The break-up of the Cold War has been disastrous for some multinational companies and their workers. The defence industries have laid off thousands of workers. Makers of submarines and planes, General Dynamics, sacked 17,000 workers in 20 months in the era of the 'new Cold War' (Juergensmeyer, 1993). Since the Berlin Wall came down, 300,000 workers have lost their jobs in the defence industry. At the same time, massive military spending raises inflation and aids the decline in economic competitivity. The nations that spent a greater share of the GNP on the military had a slower financial growth rate (nations such as Germany, Denmark, France, Austria, Belgium, Norway, Netherlands, Sweden, UK, Japan, Canada, US and Italy). Defence and military projects seem to create jobs (though without public decision or accountability), but with similar billions spent in the civil area, similar numbers of jobs would be created. For every billion dollars spent on the military in the US 9,000 jobs were lost, according to a 1982 survey.[15] One notorious aspect of employment in the defence industry is the number of retired officers (navy captains and army colonels, for example) who are given jobs.

There are 30,000-plus tactical and inter-mediate-range nuclear weapons and 20,000 strategic weapons. One Lance battlefield missile can deliver six Hiroshimas, while a submarine costs 1.5 billion dollars. These figures come from the early 1980s. Let's look at figures from the late 1980s (1989): the US had 25,000 warheads, the USSR had 25,000, the UK and France some 500, China 300 and Israel 150. The USA had 13,000 strategic warheads, the USSR 11,000 strategic warheads; the USA had 1,000 tactical warheads, the USSR had 1,500 tactical warheads. The explosive power of the USA was 6,000 megatons, of the USSR, 9,000. Total explosive power for 50,000 warheads was 15,000 megatons, or about 15,000 million tonnes of TNT, which is the equivalent of 1,250,000 Hiroshima-size bombs. After the Intermediate Nuclear Forces Treaty, it was predicted in 1989, that in Europe there would still be 4,350 NATO and US nuclear weapons, comprising: 1,700 bombs on aircraft; 200 depth charges; 700 warheads from 100 Lance launchers; 900 203mm and 750 155mm artillery warheads; and about 100 Pershing 1A warheads. British and French nuclear weapons added 1,000 warheads to this total in Europe, as well as SLBMs and ADMs (Atomic Demolition Munitions). Of the American and Soviet tactical nuclear weapons deployed in Europe in 1989, there were 108 Pershing II missiles with 108 warheads; 208 GLCMs (American Cruise) with 208 warheads; 441 SS-20 missiles with 1,300 warheads; 112 SS-4s with 112 warheads; 108 SS-12/22s (short range) weapons; 20 plus SS-23 short range weapons; 320 warheads on 36 Lance launchers; 44 French Plutons; 950 Soviet SS-21 and Frog missiles; and 7,725 Soviet Scud missiles. In 1986 50 American MX missiles were deployed, with 50 more planned; there were 100 B-1B bombers; 500 Midgetman missiles for 1992; Lance was going to be extended; a new air-to-surface missile (SRAM and SRAM-T) was planned for 1995. Before and after the INF Treaty, then, there was little reduction in the sheer numbers and power of the nuclear arsenals of the nuclear nations. In 1989 predictions for the 1995 nuclear capability included: 1,000 air-to-surface missiles; 800 surface-to-surface missiles; 600 nuclear artillery shells; 400 submarine-launched Cruise missiles; 1,000 French and British missiles; 200 naval depth charges; and 700 nuclear bombs on board aircraft. This would mean, in 1995, a total of some 5,000 nuclear warheads still in Europe.[16]

In 1995 there was around three thousand tons of highly enriched uranium. Only thirty tons of it, though, was subject to scrutiny by the IAEA (International Atomic Energy Agency). This means that the IAEA could not police 99% of highly enriched uranium. There was a thousand tons of plutonium in the world in 1995, but only a third of it was monitored by international agencies. Treaties such as the Nuclear Non-Proliferation Treaty were designed to curtail the spread of nuclear weapons, but did not (even though 140 parties signed it). There is no coherent, global policy on the control of nuclear arms, let alone universal treaties and policies for chemical, biological or missile weapons. It's difficult to see how such a tiny amount of inspectors (42 before the Gulf War) in the International Atomic Energy Agency could police the world's nuclear stockpiles. When the IAEA went to check on Sadaam Hussein's nuclear capability in Baghdad in 1990 and 1992 Iraq was declared OK. By and large, the Iraqis had shown the IAEA team what Hussein wanted them to see.[17] The stuff needed to make atomic bombs – plutonium and uranium – is relatively easily hidden. The people who steal the potentially lethal materials are often insiders, people with professional knowledge of the institutions and sites in which plutonium and uranium are kept (post-Cold War Russia is one of the nations most susceptible to nuclear theft).[18] Nuclear smugglers have been caught in Germany, Austria and Belorus: the police have recorded over 100 incidents of illegal transportation of nuclear materials.

How successful have the nuclear treaties been? Arms control has had little effect on decreasing nuclear weapons, neither has disarmament: disarmament 'has had no effect whatsoever on nuclear, conventional or chemical weapons' (Stephenson, 1983, 8). In 1958 there was the Moratorium on Nuclear Tests. But in 1962 tests started up again. The Antarctic Treaty (1959) banned nukes in the Antarctic, and has been a success. 1963 saw the Partial Test Ban Treaty, banning nuclear weapons in the sea, outer space and the atmosphere. Tests were forced underground. Since the PTB France and China have carried out atmospheric tests. The PTB has lessened nuclear pollution, but has not stopped testing. The 1963 'Hot Line' Agreement, in which the two superpowers communicated via a 'hot line', is known to have defused a Middle East crisis (in 1973). The Outer Space Treaty (1967) prevented weapons of mass destruction in space, but did not deter the superpowers from developing smaller weapons, such as lasers. It has not, of course, prevented masses of military satellites being launched. The 1967 Treaty of Tlatelolco was intended to make Latin America nuclear-free. The Non-Proliferation Treaty of 1968 aimed to curb the spread of nuclear weapons. It did not work with nations that were interested in obtaining nuclear weapons, such as non-signatories China, France, Israel, India, South Africa, Pakistan, Brazil and Argentina. The Seabed Treaty (1971), preventing nuclear arms being attached to the seabed, has worked so far. 1971's Accidents Measures Agreement aims to keep safeguards and security systems in place. Each party has to inform other nuclear parties that a nuclear accident has occurred. The Threshold Test Ban Treaty (1974) limited (underground) nuclear testing to 150 kilotons. Critics have suggested that this ban/ limit has been broken several times.

SALT I in 1972 was intended to limit the deployment of ABMs and strategic missiles. Like SALT II (1979), SALT I was one of the more controversial and much disputed nuclear treaties. For some critics, with SALT I the superpowers simply agreed to limit nuclear systems which they could not afford and which were not that effective anyway in nuclear political terms. Despite SALT I being signed, nuclear weapons productions continued, including the deadly MIRV technology. SALT II was signed by Brezhnev and Jimmy Carter, and limited the number of launchers, MIRVs and therefore warheads – but only on long-range missiles, not on tactical and theatre nuclear weapons.

For poor old Blighty, too near the Warsaw Pact countries for comfort during the Cold War, Soviet air power was fearsome. The 410 Tu-16s, 160 Tu-22s, 235 Tu-26s, 630 Su-24s, 100 Tu-95s and 43 MYA-4s add up to a terrifying amount of military force. These bombers and jets can carry hundreds of megatons of explosives.

The numbers of missiles in the mid-1980s were just as impressive: there were 224 SS-4 missiles (1 megaton yield, a range of 1,900 km, but with a 2.3 km CEP or Circular Error Probable – that is, the radius of a circle around the target inside which there's a 50% probability of the missile falling). There were 378 SS-20 missiles, with a yield of 1.5 megatons, a range of 5,000 km and a 0.4 km CEP capacity, making them much more deadly. There were 120 SS-11 missiles, with a 1 megaton yield, a range of 13,000, 10,000 and 8,800 km and a CEP of 1.1 km. The SS-19 missile, which came into service in 1982, had a very accurate 0.3 km CEP, a range of 6,200 miles and a yield of 6 x 550 kilotons (Model 1), one 5 megaton (Mod 2) or MIRV 6 x 550 kilotons (Mod 3). The SS-20 caused fear in NATO countries because it was difficult to detect, and counter-measures were ineffective. The SS-20 is a 2-stage solid-propellant missile, with 3 MIRVs, a range of 4,600 miles (SS-20 Model 3), CEP 400 metres (Model 2), payload: one 1.5 megaton (Model 1), MIRV 3 x 150 kiloton (Mod 2), one 50 Milton (Mod 3).

NUKESPEAK, NUKETALK, NUCLEAR WAR

'Nukespeak', the terminology of nuclear warfare, has its own poetry. We hear of arms escalation, ground shock, detonation, air burst, broken arrows, ground zero, maximum yield, deterrence, the sanctuary theory, overkill, overpressure, time-sensitive targets, stealth, fratricide, launch-under-attack, single-shot kill probability, first strike, AEW, CIWS, HEAT, SOSUS, MAW, WPO, NATO, ICBM, SS-20, Pershing II, BGM-1099. The phrase 'nuclear' of course chimes with 'new clear war', or perhaps 'new clear dawn'. Indeed, after a nuclear war there will be a special kind of 'new clear dawn', a sunrise on a humanmade wasteland.

The terms of nuclear war have now entered the language. People say "I feel nuclear about him" meaning they're lusting after someone. Breaking-up or an argument in romance is called fall-out. 'There's been a bit of a fall-out between them'. Making love is the meltdown. It is the ultimate fusion: the intimate, gentle darkness of two people in love and the exterior, public blinding brilliance and horror of a nuclear attack. The language of nuclear terror is appropriated by lovers and friends. In both realms of experience – nuclear war and bourgeois romance – these terms – *fall-out, meltdown, feeling nuclear* – do not describe even a billionth of the actual reality. The little word 'love' hardly even hints at the vast range of feelings lovers experience. Similarly, terms such as 'bomb' or 'fall-out' palely evoke the true horror of nuclear war. Writers of 'erotica' and pornography save a few terms up for the sex scenes, when the 'action' intensifies. Breasts become 'tits', penises become 'cocks' and the vagina is the 'cunt'. Instead of 'making love', characters 'fuck'. Advisers on 'erotica' and pornography say these 'crude', 'dirty' or 'four-letter' words have to be used in writing; there's no avoiding them, it seems.

Once this point of using the 'four-letter' words is reached, there is nowhere else to go (except perhaps into extended experimental monologues, as with Molly in *Ulysses,* or Henry Miller in his *Tropic* trilogy). Using the words 'cock', 'cunt' and 'fuck' is rock-bottom for the porn/ 'erotica' writer. (Heterosexual) couples say they use these words in bed but nowhere else. It's as if a point of no return is reached. The 'general public' knows that once a politician uses these words, her/ his credibility is destroyed. In movies, though, saying 'fucking' this, 'fucking' that is mandatory: it demonstrates that a character is *serious.* 'Like, maaan, where's my *fucking* drugs, you scum.' The word *fuck* becomes the foundation of movies such as *Pulp Fiction, Goodfellas, Platoon* and *Apocalypse Now,* because these films portray extreme situations, and 'extreme' language is required. While in films extremes of language are used to depict extremes of violent feeling (as in 'I'm gonna fuckin' kill ya, sucker'), in lovemaking the word 'fuck' or 'cunt' is a moment of disclosing one's desires. 'I want to fuck you' becomes the ultimate statement of flattery, and is valued higher in the supercynical post-1945 era than the ancient, immortal words 'I love you'.

In military or war scenarios, however, the opposite occurs: as the battle intensifies, military language becomes reduced to capitals letters (SDI, AWACS, C_2, SCUD C, ASA) or innocuous, bland terms such as 'platform' or 'AirLand battle' or C4I.[19] Tiny words such as 'hit' do for the devastation of bombs. The higher up the command hierarchy, in the war zone, the blander the terms become. Rather than the extremes of sexual or pornographic language, war and military terminology resorts to banal phrases such as 'non-lethal weapons'. The acronym for the 'no first use of nuclear weapons' policy (which NATO did not accept, while the Warsaw Pact did) is NOFUN.

For cultural critic Gayatri Chakravorty Spivak terms such as 'nuclear war' are the 'great proper names' that the liberal West bestows upon massive events of human suffering. Typical examples, Spivak suggests, are the Holocaust and Stalin. Such

naming controls and categories such events of intolerable pain.[20]
French philosopher Luce Irigaray has written:

> Huge amounts of capital are allocated to the development of death
> machines in order to ensure peace, we are told. This warlike method of
> organizing society is not self-evident. It has its origin in patriarchy. It
> has a sex. But the age of technology has given weapons of war a power
> that exceeds the conflicts and risks taken among patriarchs. Women,
> children, all living things, including elemental matter, are drawn into the
> maelstrom. (1994, 4-5)

Nuclear war, like other forms of war, does seem to be a male
preserve. Luce Irigaray writes:

> Patriarchal culture is based on sacrifice, crime and war. It is a culture
> that makes it men's duty or right to fight in order to feel themselves, to
> inhabit a place, and to defend their property, and their families and
> country as their property. (1994, 5)

NOTES

1. Sources: *The Observer Atlas of World Affairs*, Philips 1971; Ruth Leger, ed: *World Military and Social Expenditures*, World Priorities, 1982; Wilson, 1983, 36-37. The value of property destroyed in the Second World War was estimated in 1961 at $230 billion. This sum did not include the losses created by industry being diverted to the war effort. The total expenditure of belligerents in the war was estimated at $1,154 billion. (Clarke, 1982, 27)

2. See Paul Kennedy: *The Rise and Fall of the Great Powers*, Random House, New York 1987; Richard Rosecrance: *The Rise of the Trading State*, Basic, New York 1986; Edward Luttwak, 1986, and "America's Setting Sun", *The New York Times*, 23 Sept 1991, and "U.S.-Japan Treaty Can Turn Things Around", *Los Angeles Times*, 24 March 1992; C. Fred Bergsten: "The Primacy of Economics", *Foreign Policy*, Summer 1992

3. Joan Smith: "My propaganda machine is bigger than yours", *The Independent*, 3 September 1995

4. Michael Dummett: "Nuclear Warfare", in Blake, 1984, 38

5. Before Hiroshima, the Americans attacked Tokyo with 334 B-29 bombers, destroying sixteen square miles an 267,171 buildings, killing 84,000 civilians and wounding 40,000 more. (Fred Kaplan: *The Wizard of Armageddon*, Simon & Schuster, New York 1983, 42)

6. Rockwell ad, *Jane's Defence Weekly*, vol. 24, no. 7, 19 August 1995, 19

7. Rosvoorouzhenie ad, *Jane's Defence Weekly*, vol. 24, no. 7, 19 August 1995, 19

8. James Adams: "Dawn of the cyber soldiers", *Sunday Times*, 15 October 1995, 5

9. James Adams: "Day of the Pentagon mindbenders", *Sunday Times*, 3 Dec 1955, 1, 21

10. During the Falklands conflict, foreign correspondents in Britain were barred from press briefings.

11. Harvey Meieran: "Roles of Mobile Robots in Kuwait and the Gulf War", 18th Annual Technical Exhibit and Symposium, Association for Unmanned Vehicle Systems, Washington DC 1991

12. See Peter Black: "Soft Kill", *Wired*, July 1993; "New York Business Warned Over Threat of Telecoms Failure", *Financial Times*, 19 June 1990; Neil Munro: "U.S. Boosts Information Warfare Initiatives", 25 Jan 1993; John Dehaven: "Stealth Virus Attacks", *Byte*, May 1993; John Burgess: "FBI Investigates Computer Tapping in Spring Contact", *International Herald Tribune*, 22 Feb 1990

13. In the hierarchy of 'classified' papers in the US government machine, "For Official Use Only" is the least restricted category; other types include "Confidential", "Secret", "NATO Secret", "Top Secret", "SCI" ("Sensitive Compart-mented Information") and "BIGOT".

14. *Aerospace Daily*, 24 February 1983; see also Adams; G. Adams & G. Quinn: *The Iron Triangle*, Transaction, New Brunswick 1982

15. *The Costs and Consequences of Reagan's Military Build-up*, International Machinists & Aerospace Workers, AFL-C10, 1982

16. Frank Barnaby: "The Nuclear Arms Race: Running Hard", in Barnett,

16-22

17. See Diana Edensword & Fary Milhollin: "Iraq's Bomb – an Update", *New York Times*, 26 April 1993; "The Annual Report for 1990", International Atomic Energy Agency", July 1991; "The Nuclear Epidemic", *U.S. News & World Report*, 16 March 1992; J.F. Pilat: "Iraq and the Future of Nuclear Nonproliferation: The Roles of Inspections and Treaties", *Science*, 6 March 1992

18. See Steve Liesman: "Smuggler's Paradise", *Moscow Times*, 5 Dec 1992; John-Thor Dahlberg: "Ex-Soviets 'Loose Nukes' Sparking Security Concerns", *Los Angeles Times*, 28 Dec 1992

19. C4I means 'Command, Control, Communications, Computers and Intelligence'. Originally, the term 'command and control' for warfare was sufficient (known by the acronym C2). Then came 'Command, Control and Communication', or C3. Then C3I (C3 plus Intelligence). Then C4I.

20. Spivak, in *Block*, 10, 1985

II

HELL ON EARTH

HELL ON EARTH:
A NUCLEAR WAR 'WORST CASE' SCENARIO

Here's how you might die in a nuclear strike. Maximum capability is about one strategic warhead hitting a target every twenty seconds. Let's take a one megaton air-burst scenario. At ground zero, all buildings would be destroyed. Winds of 1,000 mph. There may be an 'echo' of the blast wave (the 'Mach' effect) resulting in double the overpressure. The fireball will rise at 250 feet / second, expanding to 6,000 feet diameter after ten seconds. The radioactive cloud would be 3 miles high in 30 seconds. All combustible stuff would ignite, some up to 8 miles away. Air will heat to 10,000,000° C. Heat travels outwards at 186,000 miles per second. Flesh would melt. People would die in the suffocation from the firestorm. At 1.5 miles from ground zero overpressure is 30 times than normal atmospheric pressure. From two to five miles away, most buildings would be flattened, within 15 or so seconds. Winds of 130 mph. Clothing would ignite. Radiation sickness is inevitable.

At three miles away you'll feel a flash of light (christened the *pika-don* at Hiroshima); then intense heat which chars to the bone (full-thickness burns); fifteen seconds later the windows would be blown in by the blast wave; and you'd be thrown around by the wind. First degree burns as far as 20 miles from detonation. The EMP (electromagnetic pulse) will disrupt computers, telephones, radios, radars and power supplies.

Most people would be permanently blinded by the brilliant light. There are about 200 radioactive elements in fall-out dust. Fall-out is second-stage radiation, contaminating water, the food chain, everything. Everywhere would be a 'Z Zone', a fall-out zone. Nice to know, too, that radiation is undetectable by the five senses. You may have a mortal dose and not know it. You'll know soon, though. You're in for a party, with radiation comin' at ya in 4 types: alpha, beta, gamma and neutron. Gamma rays can penetrate several inches of concrete. Strontium-90, with its beta and gamma particles, may be absorbed by the body instead of calcium: it might cause cell mutations and cancers. Uranium and plutonium isotopes are nice, affecting bones, the respiratory tract, liver, kidneys and lymphnodes: radiation lasts up to thousands of years. Ionzing radiation'll give you nausea, vomiting, diarrhoea, fever, delirium, exhaustion, haemorrhages, hair loss, ulcers, anaemia and lukaemia. Feeding is difficult, as wounds will break and become infected.

The North American Aerospace Defence Command (NORAD) at Cheyenne Mountain in Colorado will be buzzing with 24-hour activity. Joint Chiefs of Staff and the US president will be communicating via various 'hot lines'. The flying HQ may be used (the Boeing E-4B advanced airborne command post jet, with its thirteen separate radio systems broadcasting on VHF, SHF, HF, VLF and LF, its satellite dishes, its 25 onboard telephones, 12 of which have encryption facility for secure conversations, its protective thermal shielding and hardened electronics). The AABNCP flies from the Strategic Air Command's 1st Airborne

Command and Control squadron at Offutt airforce base in Nebraska, and from Andrews AFB in Virginia.

Nuclear reactors will be hit with ground-bursts: the fall-out from the cores with their long-lived radioactive isotopes, will be deadly. Not just cities but airfields, communications centres, military stores and camps will also be targets. A list of targets in the UK would include: submarines and bases, stockpiles, strategic command centres (Hawthorn, Whitehall, High Wycombe, etc), communications links (including British Telecom centres and the microwave tower network), the very low frequency radio stations at Rugby and Criggon, used for talking to submerged submarines, missile and long range radar centres (such as Clee Hill, Fyllingdales, Bishopcourt), air defence missile and interceptor bases, nuclear production sites (such as Burghfield, Aldermaston, Sellafield, Cardiff), power stations, nuclear power stations (such as Dungeness, Douunreay, Wylfa, Heysham), the chemical industries, oil and gas terminals and ports, troop concentrations (Salisbury, Aldershot, Colchester, etc), fuel depots, ammunition stocks, ports, government administration centres, and finally the major urban and industrial centres: London, Manchester, Birmingham, Leeds, Bradford, Sheffield, Southampton, Bristol, Glasgow, Dundee, Newcastle, Huddersfield, Hull, Portsmouth, Swansea, Leicester, Coventry, Liverpool, Cardiff, Nottingham, Derby and so on.

If birds are killed insects might devastate crops. Fires fanned by the winds will destroy much woodland. The 'Square Leg' operation of 1980 estimated 100 US military targets in Britain, including Upper Heyford, Boscombe Down, Greenham Common Burtonwood, etc, as well as Birmingham, Sheffield, Liverpool, Swansea, Glasgow, etc.

In Britain, there will be a million dead, three million injured. Or 35 million surviving, depending on which survey you read. Switzerland says it has shelter space for 90% of its population.

They'll be hiding in motorway tunnels. The advice the world governments have given is to dig a hole and hide in it. Or turn a room into a fall-out sanctuary, for two weeks. Or start praying.

The US will try to disperse their aircraft around the country, and many airfields will be hit. Towns such as Oxford, Cheltenham, Carlisle, Chester and Birmingham will have airburst attacks, the idea being to kill as many people as possible. Places such as Liverpool, St Mawgan, Coningsbury, Bracknell and Farnborough will receive ground bursts to knock out machinery, ports, industries, ships and buildings. Places like Felixstowe and Canvey Island will have ten times more bombers attacking them than, say, Swindon or Manchester. The Clyde and the Forth will be blown to smithereens.

Ships such as aircraft carrier HMS Hermes will be bombed out of the water immediately, along with the 90,000-ton nuclear-powered *Enterprise*-Class super aircraft carriers, and the *Kiev*-Class with its SS-N-12 surface-to-surface missiles.

And don't forget chemical, biological and radiological warfare. You'll need NBC-protective clothing. For example, the nerve agent GB incapacitates quickly; if inhaled death follows in a few minutes. Sarin nerve gas causes sweating, cramps, defecation, coma and convulsion. Hydrogen cyanide or 'blood gas' blocks respiration. Mustard or blister gas causes broncho-phneumonia. BZ is a (discontinued) psychedelic aerosol causing hallucination and disorientation. CN, CS and CR are tear gases, causing burning, nausea, difficult respiration and tears. 2, 4-D and 2, 4, 5-T are defoliants which kill vegetation.[1] Although 120 nations met in 1993 in Paris to sign the Chemical Weapons Convention, the Arab League did not sign, and the Russians continued to develop chemical weapons. Russia also developed biological weapons (such as the 'super plague') for years after the 1972 treaty designed to terminate biological warfare.[2]

The 'H-hour' approacheth.

Think of the people manning those lonely snowbound DEW (Distant Early Warning) radar sites at Cambridge Bay and Dye Main in Canada or Thule in Greenland. This is their big hour, the fruit of all those years spent watching for enemy missiles. Others are monitoring the PARCS (Perimeter Acquisition Radar Attack Characterization System), the PAVE-PAWS (Phased Array Radar for SLBM Detection), the SPADATS at Cheyenne Mountain, Colorado (Space Surveillance System), the JASS (Joint Air Surveillance System) and the BMEWS (Ballistic Missile Early Warning System). Other warning stations include NAVSPASUR in south-east USA; the USAF's 496L 'Spacetrack' system in Turkey, Italy, New Zealand, New Brunswick, New Mexico, California, Hawaii and South Korea; the 414L system (in 1983 this was two back-scatter 'over-the-horizon' radars at Maine); and the CADIN/ Pinetree Line. Britain's own BMEWS station at Fyllingdales, Yorkshire, will do its bit too, although it's been superceded. The US satellites will be the first to pick up the heat traces as the missiles launch.

The Attack Warning Red signal will come from the Home Office Warning Officer at High Wycombe. The signal is given to police, HQs and warning points (there were 19,000 warning points in the UK in 1985, consisting of coastguard, police and fire stations, hospitals, civil and military centres, industrial centres, shops, pubs and private houses).[3] Also to the BBC, who'll be in their broadcasting bunker at Wood Norton near Evesham, just as in the Second World War. The UKWMO centre (UK RAOC) will collate data from radar, Airborne Early Warning, BMEWS and other sources, before alerting the 250 Carrier Control Points and the 7,000 powered sirens and the 11,000 warning points in rural areas.

The old attack scenarios (Square Leg, Scrum Half, Hard Rock and other 'war games' exercises) suggest that about 300 megatons will be used on Britain. But the Soviets have over 600 megatons for the UK.₄ Three thousand megatons could be used in a 'worse case' scenario.

Nuclear devices have been used now in Germany, the Gulf, Central America, Afghanistan, New Zealand, Russia, the Pacific, etc. What will a nuclear war/ attack/ strike/ accident be like? Hiroshima and Nagasaki provide the only real-life reference-points for what atomic bombs can do. At 8.15 am on 6 August 1945, there were the 'pika' (flash of light), the wave of heat, the 'don' (thunder of the detonation) and suddenly utter chaos. Afterwards, a park covered with corpses waiting to be cremated; casualties staggering about; children with skin as well clothes peeling off their bodies; dense clouds of smoke; buildings on fire; electricity poles on fire. One eyewitness said: 'I had never seen anything which resembled it before, but I thought that should there be a hell, this was it.'₅

The nuclear assault on Britain and Europe will occur at two or three a.m., the dead time. Every kind of warhead will be used: SS-18, T4, CC-NX-4, SS-NX-20, MSBS-20. Total world nuclear delivery in the full-scale exchange will be between 30,000 and 50,000 megatons. In other words, maximum blackout, a comprehensive wipeout that will destroy every city, town and village, and all livestock, plantcrop and animal kingdoms of the world.

The chances of survival in the open are minimal, on any of the Western continents. Winds and atmospheric changes will send radiation around the globe within ten days, with levels in excess of 500 rads. This'll kill half the population in the long term. Blast waves and heat flashes will create firestorms over major cities and computer/ missile emplacements. Ground shocks will cause major earthquakes and tectonic shifts.

There are over 20,000 targets, some soft, some hard. In the panic of the exchange, major computer communications centres will be demolished. Without higher command, the military groups will make many mistakes.⁶ Nations aiming to hit Europe (may) include Iran, Libya, Russia, India, South Africa and Argentina. The colonial countries will hit back at their one-time colonizers.

In the panic to disarm and depth-charge submarines there will be dog-fights between bombers and jets, satellites and head-quarters of nuclear nations. In the collisions that ensue, some subs will be destroyed, leaking out radiation into the oceans, in all directions. The blast waves and heat flashes on the West Coast of America will constitute a holocaust in themselves, making a molten mass of atomic energy. New York and Washington will receive at least ten missiles each, some from pirate submarines in the Arctic ocean. Moscow will be sunk under at least fifteen megatons. As many command centres surround Moscow itself, many of these will be knocked out. More mistakes will be made. Some missiles will explode on the home-sender's ground. As delivery systems, in the form of bombers, satellites, submarines and underground silos, are overloaded with cross-referenced targets, confusions will ensure ignition and targetting mistakes. There will be faulty launches and some missiles will explode in their silos.

Launch mode is hot.

The number of people killed instantly will be about a thousand million or more. The number of people killed in the next hour after detonation will be approximately 600 million. In the next five hours, over two-thirds of human life will be dead or dying. After two weeks the number of people surviving is estimated at about two hundred million. Of these only twenty million will be alive after six weeks.

If the world leaders and politicians were evacuated to the Moon, they will be looking at a planet which will have been subjected to about thirty thousand nuclear explosions. There is a star in the galaxy for every person ever lived on Earth, they say. And there is a fragment of a nuclear explosion for every person living on Earth now. Every human being will receive their own dose of the Holocaust.

With the huge amount of nuclear megatons being exploded in such a short time (two or three hours) the effects on the atmosphere and ecosphere are hard to predict. All animals apart from insects will be destroyed, or fatally wounded. The soil will become barren. The power-failures will mean even more mistakes in the launch centres. The communications network, which has powered the planet with news and decisions for decades, will be destroyed overnight. Impossible to say what the consequences of the destruction of America's agriculture will be, which is exported in vast quantities to Russia, Europe and the Third World. Without any clear picture of the situation, no nation will be able to decide on the next course of action. There will be no burial of the dead, for instance.

Bombers which have delivered warheads may be able to ride the blast waves, but they will return to airfields decimated by the enemy. Warships will be the first hit by marauding enemy fighters. No frigates or aircraft carriers will survive the first hour of the exchange. Submarines will survive, but no dockyards will be left after the first hour. All airports, harbours, shipyards, silos, bunkers, command centres and sub-arctic bases will be the first targets of any force.

Some areas, in which nuclear bombs will be detonating simultaneously, will become pure firestorms: North Europe, the Far East, the Gulf and the Levant, European Russia, the West and East Coasts of America. Even the deepest fall-out shelters and bunkers will be smothered by flying debris from five hundred or more major cities as they are vaporized. Billions of kilograms of fission and fusion. A million out-of-bounds zones. One gigantic waste land.

If the above attack scenario seems unreal, or unlikely, or overwhelming, let's take a smaller ('limited') nuclear strike on Britain. How many megatons do you want? Many scenarios postulate 2-300 for the UK, but 60-90 would be sufficient to ruin the country. In the run-up to the attack, there would be a 'war scare' situation: the police would round up political 'subversives', prisons would be vacated to house them. The police would act on information housed by the police's national computer at Hendon. It's not clear what special forces such as the SAS would be doing.[7] Transport and key sites would be requisitioned, to provide support for the military (ships, railways, roads, ports, commercial aircraft). The police would be involved in maintaining law and order, doling out petrol, keeping Essential Service Routes clear. Instead of following the 'stay put' policy, many people would protest – up to a quarter of Londoners said they would be prepared to use direct forms of protest; about 12% of people would be prepared to consider violent means of protest – quite different from the handful of political 'agitators' which the government perceives. In the worsening international crisis, people would be stocking up on food, many would try to leave built-up areas; a third of Londoners, for example, would try to get out of the city. In a 'war scare' situation, hardly anybody would bother turning up to work. Cities would therefore be severely disrupted even before the war started.

Aggressive actions by one nation would be followed by counteractions; trying to keep every operation covert would eventually become impossible. For example, build-ups of shipping would be hard to mask. The increase in ships at sea, the change in the patterns of commercial shipping, the deployment of surveillance craft, and the increase in activity around dockyards would become obvious. Nations would try to protect their merchant shipping; the submarines that were shadowing aircraft carriers would be targeted in an effort to pre-empt their attacks; waters such as the Icelandic Channel, the Caribbean, the Black Sea, off South-

East Asia, the Panama Canal, the Red Sea, the Persian Gulf, around Western Europe and Japan would become a hive of activity, communication, and attacks.

Submarines would be major targets, and, once detected, would have nuclear depth charges launched against them. Because they're so mobile as nuclear missile launchers, a primary aim of every major navy will be to find and destroy nuclear submarines. For Britain the Greenland-Iceland-UK (GIUK) gap is crucial, and must be carefully patrolled, to stop Russian subs moving into the Atlantic. In the late 1980s, Russia had some 300 submarines fitted with conventional weapons. At this time there were at least 6 nuclear-powered submarines of a new class, and ten classes of older attack submarines (of which 8 were nuclear-powered). The GIUK gap would be electronically bugged – keeping tabs on Russian subs would be a crucial task.

Parts of the Greenland gap are mined, with CAPTOR mines. Not only is the Greenland-Iceland-UK gap bugged with hydrophones on the seabed (the SOSUS – Sound Surveillance System), but the Kamchatka Peninsula, both of America's coasts, the eastern Atlantic and the mouth of the Mediterranean are also bugged. NATO will be keeping an optical, infra-red and radar eye on the movements of the Soviet Navy Northern Fleet – its HQ is at Severomorsk, with bases on the Kola Peninsula at Motovskij Gulf, Polyarny, Archangelsk and Severodvinsk. Helicopters and ships will trail sonars, jets will track subs, as will satellites – all part of the ASW (Anti-Submarine Warfare) system.

Among the many things that an enemy would be trying to do would be to jam early warming systems and communications, to spoof anti-aircraft systems, listen in to radio and telephone conversations, disrupt radio traffic, and 'hide' the flights, electronically, of their bombers. Special electronic warfare jets would fly with bombers and fighters during sorties to confuse and jam enemy aircraft.

In the run-up to the nuclear war, the social and political fabric would decay. For example, people would pull out all their savings to buy food and supplies; but there would be a fixed amount of commodities on offer, leading to an inflationary situation. The state support system could be disrupted as managerial, administrative and professional groups leave the urban areas. Unemployment would rise if the international crisis continued; the vulnerable – ethnic minorities, single parent families, the unskilled – would become increasingly vulnerable. Tensions would rise. Children would not go to school. Long-established institutions (health, education, social security) would be weakened. Social focal points, such as schools, work, pubs, would be under threat, and would disappear after an attack. Transport in the rubble-strewn city would be very difficult. Law and order would decline, as would forms of personal protection.

Many people would suffer disaster syndrome, and possibly withdraw further from (what would be left of) society.[8] Racial tensions would probably increase. Some people would not be able to afford to evacuate urban zones, further exacerbating social tension. As food, fuel and shelter become eagerly sought-after, not only battles but more deaths would ensue: many would not have the money to buy much-needed supplies.

Thousands of people (or millions, depending on the scale of the attack) would be in shock, in 'disaster syndrome', while others would be at the top of the anxiety curve. With EMP disabling communications, there would not only be a news black-out, just when people would be extremely desperate for news, but no all-clear signal. Only radio will be maintained after an attack, according to the Home Office. With no media information, and with telephones and communications down, obtaining hard facts on the situation would be difficult for many people. Rumour and speculation and anxiety would be rife; confusion would be the most common state of mind. Oscillating from despair to 'community spirit' would be typical, with any number of personal problems painfully accentuated. Preventing people from evacuating cities would create much tension, although the Home Office has stated that no one would be stopped from leaving built-up areas. However, with up to a third of people in the capital saying in a survey they'd leave London in a nuclear war, that might mean anything up to 3 million people trying to get out of London, which would be chaos.

Transport services would be severely disrupted: supply of water, electricity, gas, etc, would be damaged. Many establishments, from offices to shops and factories, would be forced to close. With even a small attack on the capital (four nuclear bombs, say) all rescue and medical systems would not be able to cope.[9] There would be spreads of disease by the partial collapse of the water and sewage systems. A quarter of the city's housing would be uninhabitable. Clearing the rubble from the city's roads and railway lines would take 1-2 years. In a 30 megaton attack on the UK, there would be 8.3 million casualties in Britain. It would take 15-20 years to clear the debris from the roads and railways.

There would be 750,000 corpses to bury immediately following the attack. There would be no gas, water or electricity for the public. London and other cities might be flooded as rivers broke their banks. London's electricity capital, sub-station and transformer stations would be affected by floods. Without electricity, many homes in a Winter attack would become extremely uncomfortable. Parts of the Underground would not flood, but much would stay flooded afterwards.

If there were high altitude exo-atmospheric explosions there would be a strong electromagnetic pulse (EMP) over the country.[10] This would knock out gas and electricity supplies. It would also affect water supplies, as most waterworks are run by electricity. Water systems might be melted by fires spreading from the rupture of chemical stores. Reservoirs and rivers might be damaged and contaminated. Water-borne diseases might spread (typhoid, poliomyelitus, food poisoning and diarrhoea, for example). After the attack, and due to radiation, there would be factors to deal with such as bad diet, loss of acquired immunity, overcrowding and contaminated water. Fun things to do would be dealing with the dead.

In the Second World War there were between 70,000 and 80,000 bodies decomposing in the ruins of German cities after the end of the war. In Hamburg 10,000 bodies were unrecovered 2 years after the Allied bombings. In Manila, at the end of WW II, American soldiers were unable to work on mass burials for more than a week at a time because of nausea, vomiting, depression, anorexia, nightmares and insomnia. In the Philippines, it took eighty men supervised by 1 officer eight weeks to bury 39,000 dead.[11] After a ten megaton nuclear attack on London there would be about six million dead. Burying the corpses would be low down on the priorities of the survivors for a time, and it would take months even with a coordinated effort (if this were possible after a ten megaton attack). World War Two not only saw six million dying in the Holocaust, but fifteen million soldiers and nearly twice that figure among civilians were killed.

Nuclear air bursts would destroy much of Britain's communications network. Only a few communications centres are hardened against electromagnetic pulses (partly because of the cost). Communications that are still plugged in to an aerial, power source or land line are the most affected by EMPs, so the Home Office advises such equipment should be disconnected. However, a war situation is precisely the point at which communication is absolutely essential. Communication centres of national security, such as the Home Office Central Communications Establishment at Harrow and the air defence and air traffic control centre at West Drayton, would be among the first targets, even in a relatively small (4 megaton) nuclear strike. In a 90+ megaton scenario, no telephone headquarters would remain, and half the telephone exchanges would be destroyed. Microwave communications, satellite dishes, cable TV, and most radio masts would be destroyed. Even a 'small' attack (say, ten cities) may be enough to persuade the British administration to surrender. After all, there would be a casualty list far surpassing that of the two World Wars put together. And sustained in just a few minutes.

TARGETS IN BRITAIN

Targets in Britain would include primary nuclear targets: medium and intermediate range missiles and submarine bases, long-range strike aircraft and bases, nuclear storage sites and command and communication centres. Tactical nuclear targets would include tactical aviation, carriers and bases, short-range cruise and ballistic missiles, and command and control centres. A third group of targets would include: ground forces, operational and strategic reserves, non-nuclear dumps and arms, petrol and oil sites, and naval bases. A fourth group would be air defence airfields and missile centres. A fifth group would include political, administrative, military and industrial centres, and key transportation points.

Military munitions and hardware factories would be targets, such as (in 1982) the nuclear arms complex at Burghfield (near Reading), Hawker Siddeley (in Manchester and Bolton), British Aircraft Corporation (in Luton and Preston), and Westland (in Yeovil). If Britain's industry was to be destroyed power sources and suppliers (such as power stations, oil and gas terminals) would be targets. Destroying communications and transport links, such as roads or railways, would not be cost-effective, requiring massive amounts of weaponry. In 1975 about half the power supply of the UK was produced by the twenty-five largest power stations Thus, with just 36 warheads 56% of Britain's power supply could be destroyed (Ikle, 1958, 140). An effective way for an enemy to kill many British people would be to detonate many water-bursting devices around the British Isles. With the right weather conditions, the fall-out would be deadly. This method would leave buildings nearly unaffected, so they could be used at a later date (Clarke, 159)

A likely time for the attack is mid-winter, when nations are at their weakest. A winter attack might mean that crops may not be able to recover, and that people would die when deprived of heat. A likely time of day for the attack is between three and seven in the morning in Washington DC, between 8 a.m. and noon European time. Christmas Day is likely, for obvious reasons, as is a day of bad weather. This would probably be an optimum attack time. Another propitious time might be 5 a.m. on a Sunday or a holiday morning in Summer, when troops would be on holiday, and tourists would be cluttering up Europe's roads.[12]

An eight megaton nuclear attack on Britain by Russia (in a 1986 scenario) might involve twenty Tu-26 *Backfire* bombers armed with AS-4 *Kitchen* missiles (200 kiloton yield, 0.5-1.5 km CEP) approaching Britain from the North-West using ECM and ECCM equipment to confuse and jam interceptors.

The first group of four bombers goes for Stornoway airbase, then to Upper Heyford and Lakenheath. Other groups of four Tu-26 *Backfires* attack Finningley, Scampton, Machrihanish, Wittering, Greenham Common, Kinloss, Gare Loch, Rosyth, Farnborough, Marham, Honington, Lakenheath, Molesworth and Boscombe Down, while the fifth group goes for the submarine bases at Holy Loch and Faslane.

In a thirty megaton nuclear attack on Britain 81 SS-20 missiles might be used carrying 243 warheads, and targetting the sites listed above, as well as West Drayton, Stanmore, Heathrow, Hillingdon, Saxa Vord, Lossiemouth, Buchan, Leuchars, Glasgow airport, Prestwick, Broughton Moor, Teeside Airport, Fyllingdales, Topcliffe, Elvington, Saxton Wold, Criggion, Shawbury, Speke airport, Donnington, Waddington, Cottesmore, East Midlands airport, West Raynham, Brawdy, Cheltenham, Clee Hill, Pershore, Coventry and Birmingham airports, Mildenhall, Wyton, Brompton, Bentwaters, Brize Norton, Croughton, Woodbridge, Barry Island, Bristol and Luton airports, Yeovilton, Kemble, Fairford, Welford, Abingdon, Gosport, Wilton, Gatwick, Dover, St Mawgan, Plymouth, Devonport, Exeter airport, Portland, Poole, Hurn, Ventnor and Chatham. These are just some of the targets in a 30 megaton nuclear attack.

In a 90 megaton nuclear attack on Britain, the targets would include all of the above, plus a host of other targets. For example, a one megaton warhead would hit each of the following locations: the City of London, Kingston, Whitehall, Hampstead, Enfield, Clapham, Euston, Hackney and Sutton; 150 kiloton yield warheads would go for the Firth of Clyde, Turnhouse, Eaglescliff, Leeming, Forest Moor, North Coates, Liverpool, Bawtry, Binbrook, Watton, Cranwell, Digby, Defford, Brize Norton, Feltwell, Chicksands, Stansted, Hatfield, Bawdsey, Felixstowe, Chivenor, St Athan, Cranfield, Cardiff, Filton, Kemble, Oakhanger, Benson, Bramley, Hythe, West Dean and Manston; the following places would each receive a one megaton yield warhead (an airburst at 8,200 feet, to maximize casualties): Aberdeen, Dundee, Glasgow (2 megatons), Sheffield, Birmingham (3 or 4 megatons), Leeds, Bradford, Liverpool, Newcastle (2 megatons) Greenock, Perth, Crewe, Coventry, Cheltenham, Cardiff (2 megatons) Swansea, Reading, Aylesbury, Swindon,

Watford, Guildford, Hawthorn, Stockton, Preston, Caterick, Manchester (2 or 3 megatons), Belfast, Bulford, Bracknell, Exeter, Yeovil, Colchester, Chelmsford, Stevenage, Leicester, Shrewsbury, Wolverhampton, Nottingham, Blackpool, Barrow and Rochdale.

NUCLEAR WINTER: THE AFTERMATH

If the attack occurred in Summer, it could become Winter very quickly, with temperatures reaching freezing. With a 90 megaton attack on Britain, 85-90% of people would be killed or injured. Fires would rage unchecked. Most houses would be uninhabitable; of those still standing, most would have damaged roofs, floors and walls. Wind speed and direction would be an important factor. In an 8 megaton attack on nuclear sites in the UK there might be 858,000 casualties in conditions of a wind speed of 24 km per hour in the South South-West. In a West South-West wind, however, the number of casualties rises to 905,000. In a 31 megaton nuclear attack on Britain half a million more people would be killed if the wind was from West South-West instead of the North by North-West (Steadman, 1986).

Immediately after the attack, and for some time, the priorities of the survivors would be food, water and shelter. So urgent would be the necessity for obtaining basic supplies, survivors might not have the time, energy or inclination to rebuild social structures.[13] 90 megatons would create 27 million causualties in Britain and the survivors would have full disaster syndrome. It would probably be very cold after a nuclear attack. Temperature drops of 5° C can have severe effects for the natural world, let alone humanity.

This is the so-called 'nuclear winter', which, if it occurred over a growing season, could reduce agricultural production to nearly zero. A 'nuclear winter' in the summer could be disastrous. In a Northern summer it might prevent the warming of Asian sub-continent, subverting the monsoon and creating a drought. With dense clouds of smoke thrown up into the atmosphere, temperatures might drop to near-freezing for weeks afterwards. No one knows exactly what the nuclear winter will do to the environment. There may be snow in any season, reduced light levels, and torrential rain. A January nuclear attack would create near-zero temperatures for 3 months, with 4° drops in Spring and Summer. An April war would mean temperature falls of 3° C, and average temperatures would not get higher than 10° C for the first year. In July, there is a drop of about 12° C. In October temperatures would be under 5° C for half a year. With nitrogen oxide being cast up into the stratosphere, ozone depletion is another problem: a drop of 55% could occur in the 1st year after a war, with a consequent increase in ultraviolet radiation of 100%.[14]

One assumption is that the survivors of a nuclear war would resort to a 'mediaeval' form of life, yet there would a lack of factors that made life in the Middle Ages possible: uncontaminated food, social stability, the knowledge and skills needed for survival, and a clean environment.[15]

It is not certain that people will panic *en masse*. Panic looks good in nuclear holocaust movies, but did not occur after Hiroshima or Nagasaki, or in other massively bombed locations in the Second World War (such as Hamburg, Frankfurt and Tokyo). People might not instantly become panic-stricken. Immediately after the attack, priorities such as personal security and obtaining supplies will take over. Some people did act 'like wolves and foxes to stay alive' after Nagasaki, and were 'unashamed of doing wrong, mean things'.[16] Of course there will always be some people who will try to exploit the carnage. With the 'death taboo' smashed, some people may be willing to kill for key supplies. Shock and 'freezing' may be more likely, with people unsure about outside events; they would be so concerned with adjusting to the post-attack life there may not be much concerted group activity.

Nuclear shelter life will not easy. Not knowing what the hell is going on around the world will increase the sense of isolation and deprivation. Radiation is invisible: there will not appear to be any danger out there. There may be fantasies of outsiders threatening to break into the shelter. Physical sickness will be rife, as well as hunger and thirst. Conditions will be difficult to predict (Frank, 1967, 157), but they will certainly be poor, as survivors get to grips with vomiting and diarrhoea, hours of silence, and widespread death. If between five and ten million die in and just after the attack, every survivor will know someone who's died.

Death will be everywhere, in short. Instead of something hidden away in white, clinical morgues, hospitals, body-bags and funeral parlours, death will be brazenly and disturbingly out in the open. There may be bodies everywhere. The psychological stress people will be existing under in their bunkers and damaged houses will be immense. The only example available of shelter life in Britain is again the Second World War, but that was only for limited period in which the all-clear was definitely given and understood. After the attack, there will be no all-clear for perhaps weeks. There will be no definite end to the post-attack shelter life, no resolution, no victory, but maybe a slow and painful re-building. Hunger and thirst will be norms, with no let-up for weeks or months. The stockpiles of food, maintained by the Ministry of Agriculture and Fisheries, consisting of flour, sugar, margarine, yeast and biscuits, will not constitute a basic diet, and will not last very long. Further, it is not certain who will be delivering food, nor how.

There may be little or no government immediately after the attack. Disorganization would be the norm (Ikle, 183). Even when it operates in peacetime, government, at a local or national level, depends upon a complex web of processes. An authoritarian regime seems likely after the attack for some commentators, with the regional centres controlling items such as food distribution. What's left of the military and police would probably assist in maintaining authority. Liberal systems such as democracy or socialism would probably not be restored for a while.

The population of Britain may drop dramatically – not a 'baby boom' but a 'baby vacuum', as pregnant women die and the survivors suffer abortions. The foetus is 20-60 times more susceptible to radiation than the normal adult. For months and perhaps years afterwards people may not wish to create families. Consequently, the population of Britain years after a major nuclear attack may dwindle to ten million. This might enable Britain to build its economy from what might seem like nearly nothing. Instead of relying on imports, the UK might become a self-contained agricultural nation, devoted to post-attack survival.

After a year radiation will not be a problem, and the death rate will slow down. External aid might not be forthcoming. It was important for post-Second World War Britain, and the lack of it will be serious. Three to six months after the attack may be the low point, socially and psychologically. National food stockpiles will be zero. With large parts of Britain's countryside irradiated, food will be contaminated, but people will still eat it, and die in the long term. Little of society after a nuclear attack would be recognizable. Some commentators reckon that people would have lost faith in systems of authority, self-discipline, the ability to control the environment, and the myriad forms of social cohesion.[17] The complex interrelationships of society would be destroyed overnight. While the physical effects of a nuclear war can be reasonably accurately gauged (how many houses smashed, how many people killed), the psychological effects are far harder to predict – and, perhaps, more important.

'The human race has no experience remotely comparable to full scale nuclear warfare'. Thus, Ira Lowry (1966, 6). No one's sure if nuclear bombardment will secure 'victory' for any side. Billions of pounds of TNT explosive was dropped on the Allies' enemies in the Second World War, but it was inefficient. Ten billion pounds of TNT *should* have meant the death of everyone. Similarly, 25 billion pounds of TNT were dropped during the Vietnam War, which works out at 730 pounds for each individual in 34 million. Yet it didn't kill enough people.[18] It is remarkable how seemingly devastated countries re-build themselves, like Russia after the war. 66% of Russia's occupied territories' wealth was lost in World War Two (27% of Russia's total wealth). In Eastern Europe there were 25 million dead, but the area recovered. Instead of looking back to WW 2 as a model for nuclear war, it offers insights to go back to the mediaeval era and the Black Death. In three years, between 1348 and 1350, Europe's population was cut by a quarter. After a generation, it fell by 40%. Yet Europe recovered. Similarly, a nation might recover after a nuclear war – the resilience of humans mustn't be underestimated.

NOTES

1. Julian Perry Robinson: "The Changing Status of Chemical and Biological Warfare", in *SIPRI Yearbook*, 1982
2. Toffler, 1994, 158; "Chemical Disarmament and International Security", *Adelphi Papers*, 267, International Institute for Strategic Studies
3. *Civil Defence and the Farmer*, Ministry of Agriculture, Fisheries and Food, 1985
4. Outside of Warsaw Pact nations, countries would need nuclear weapons with ranges of over 1,500 km to hit the UK. Iraq and Israel, for example, are within 5,000 km. Israel has no long-range bombers. Iraq (in 1986) supposedly had 7 Tu-22 *Blinders* and 8 Tu-16 *Badgers*. But with ranges of 2,800 and 2,400 km (respectively) they would not be able to attack the UK. Libya has 7 Tu-22 *Blinder* jets, but does not have a nuclear capability.
5. R.J. Lifton: *Death in Life: Survivors of Hiroshima*, Random House, New York 1967; Ehrlich, 189
6. During the Cuban missile crisis at least two people in the American command group were 'overcome by stress'. (Phil Williams: *GLAWARS Task 1: Crisis Management and Civil Defence*, South Bank Polytechnic 1986
7. Britain's Special Air Force has counterparts in many nations. America has its Delta Force, the US Army's First Special Forces Operational Detachment, which carries out hostage operations. The Air Force and Navy also have their own Special Operations forces. Russia has Spetsnaz, France the First and Second Parachute Brigades, and the 13th Dragoons Parachute Regiment. In 1989 estimates were that the Russian Spetsnaz force included 41 independent companies, 16-24 independent brigades, 4 naval brigades, 20 intelligence units, 3 diversionary regiments and many foreign saboteurs which could carry out Spetsnaz orders.
8. James Thompson: *GLAWARS Task 4: The Behaviour of Londoners in a Future Major War*, South Bank Polytechnic 1986
9. The British Medical Association said in 1981 that just one bomb of the size used at Hiroshima over a British city would completely overwhelm the medical services in the whole country. An attack of 200 megatons would equal 15,000 Hiroshima bombs, or forty times all the conventional explosives used in WW 2. 'The NHS could not deal with the casualties that might be expected following the detonation of a single one megaton bomb over the UK' (*The Medical Effects of Nuclear War*, Board of Science and Education of the British Medical Association, Wiley, 1981, 124). A report by the Royal College of Nursing said that '[t]he immediate effects of a nuclear war are impossible to predict, but all the adjectives of doom in the English language would hardly do justice to the effects of a nuclear strike involving *one* major weapon.' (*Nuclear War Civil Defence Planing: The Implications for Nursing*, Royal College of Nursing, 1983, 29-30)
10. The US Navy used 'non-nuclear electromagnetic pulse warheads' on their Tomahawk cruise missiles to disable Iraqi electronic systems in the Gulf War.
11. G.L. Orth: "Disaster and Disposal of the Dead", *Military*

*Medicine,*124, 1959. The ratio of military to civilian casualties in the First World War was 20 : 1. In WW 2 it was equal. In the Korean War it was 1 : 5. In Vietnam 1 : 20. In a nuclear war it could be 1 : 100 (Dewar, 1989, 33).

12. Robert Close: *The Guardian*, 11 January 1977

13. Peter Nordlie: "Societal Recovery', in Wigner, 1969, 299

14. National Academy of Sciences: *The Effects on the Atmosphere of a Nuclear Exchange*, NAS, Washington DC 1985. See also R.P. Turco *et al*: "Nuclear winter, global consequences of multiple nuclear explosions", *Science*, 222, 4630, 1983; C. Covey *et al*: "Global atmospheric effects of massive smoke injections from a nuclear war", *Nature*, 308, 1984; P.J. Crutzen & J.W. Birks: "The atmosphere after a nuclear war: twilight at noon", *Ambio*, 11, 2-3, 1982; A. Robock: "Snow and ice feedbacks prolong the effects of a nuclear winter", *Nature*, 310, 1984

15. *Nuclear War Civil Defence Planing: The Implications for Nursing*, Royal College of Nursing, 1983, 29-30

16. T. Nagai: *We of Nagasaki*, Meredith Press, New York 1969, 118

17. Kate Soper: "Human Survival", in Blake, 1984, 95-97

18. F.D. Kohler, Foreword, in L. Goure: *War Survival in Soviet Strategy*, Centre for Advanced International Studies, Miami, 1976, xv

Nuclear bomb test, New Mexico

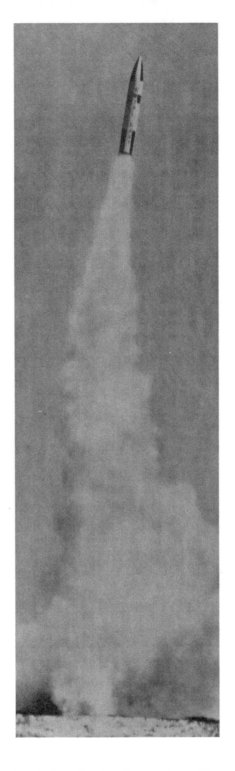

Missile launch test of the British Polaris system at Cape Kennedy

Soviet submarine, Echo II class

British nuclear submarines: the Courageous, above,
and the RN Revenge in Scotland, 1981, below.

Briitain's military naval ports:
Devonport dockyard above, with the Amazon,
and the submarine base at Plymouth, below

Images of the British Sea Harrier:
a NATO exercise with a Russian Bear-D aircraft, above,
and FRS 1 planes, below (British Aerospace)

Britain's Royal Navy vessels:
HMS Invincible, below, and with the Ark Royal, above

US Navy aircraft: Lockheed Vikings, below,
and Grauman A-6 Intruders, above.

The US air force in Vietnam: Phantom F4B, 1965, above,
and a T-37 trainer, 1967, below.

III

AMERICA GOES NUCLEAR

I can go into my office and pick up the telephone and in twenty-five minutes seventy million people will be dead.

President Nixon (in Nield, 135)

AMERICA GETS NUCLEAR

The era of the Cold War was, for the West, often perceived as 'us and them', the good, 'free', 'democratic', liberal West against the evil, dour, Communist East. The Americans were portrayed as the freedom-loving Yanks, while the Russians were the Communist Ruskies. Yet, for four years North America was the only nuclear nation. In those years, the United States was 'engaged in full-scale, unrestrained production and stockpiling of atomic bombs'. The US military ringed the Soviet Union with over 400 major military bases and 3,000 secondary bases, which were sited throughout Europe, Iceland and Greenland, the Middle East, southwest Asia, the Pacific, Alaska and Canada. This was the era of the American bombers – B-29s, B-36s, B-47s and B-52s. One B-52 bomber can carry explosives equivalent to 3,000 Hiroshimas.

It was largely the Americans who accelerated the nuclear arms race. All the time, the US propaganda machine blamed the Russians for having this or that weapon, so America must have something equivalent or as a counter-measure. Russia was seen as the enemy which was arming itself with ever-greater weapons. In fact, it was the Americans who took the lead in the development of atomic weapons, it was Americans who first developed and tested the atomic bomb, who first used the atomic bomb in a war situation, who developed the hydrogen bomb, who introduced the multiple warhead, who created the nuclear submarine with its MIRVs (multiple independently targeted re-entry vehicles), who invented MARVs (manœuvring re-entry vehicles), who first produced the neutron bomb, who invented the cruise missile, and who were adamant that they reserved the right for 'first use'.[1]

It is worth noting that the US is the only country that has used nuclear weapons – and used them in a war, aggressively, not in defence, used them against a nation that did not have nuclear arms. After the war President Truman said in a speech that God was wise to give nuclear arms to a country that was too humane to use them.

The Cuban missile crisis shook up the superpowers, and America agreed to withdraw its medium-range missiles from Turkey. These were minimal moves, though, compared to the enormity of the rest of the arms race. America was still exploring all manner of military projects. Among the most far-fetched was the Orion spaceship. America spent seven years developing a nuclear-powered battle station, with defensive 'pusher plates' which would withstand megaton detonations 500 feet away, and directional antimissile nailer explosives.

Another secret weapon was the thermonuclear-pumped X-ray laser. An atomic bomb detonates a hydrogen bomb in order to 'pump' X-ray lasers with a very long-range. Billions of dollars were injected into weapons research in the early 1980s: thus the peaceful exploration of space was essentially killed off. NASA said that 'the space science program has been almost destroyed.'[2]

In the era of the 1980s and the 'AirLand battle' scenario, the New Maritime Strategy meant that the 15 carrier-group, 600 ship US Navy would become a carrier-based nuclear airstrike capability. Instead of escorting ships across the Atlantic, the US Navy would be directly targeting Russia and Russia's missile-bearing submarines in a first strike attack plan. A variant on the US AirLand battle strategy was a NATO Follow On Force which would involve a deep strike into enemy territory, including the first use of nuclear weapons.[3] The successor to AirLand Battle, AirLand Operation, became official US doctrine on 1 August 1991: again, pre-emptive manœuvres are suggested. Later versions of army doctrine argued for forces based in America that could travel to conflicts, instead of having bases around the world. The army strategy also involved anti-drugs, civil disturbance, peace-keeping and disaster aid.

AMERICA IN BRITAIN

As far as NATO and the US is concerned, Britain was and is an 'unsinkable aircraft carrier', or in military terms, a 'forward strike base'. (America's nuclear weapons are stockpiled around the world – not only in Britain, but in Turkey, Greece, Germany, Italy and Belgium). Indeed, if one looks at the deployment of US bases in Britain (up until the early 1990s), one saw that most of them were in the East of the country, all positioned for sorties to the Soviet Union. Upper Heyford, Alconbury, Lakenheath, Bentwaters and Mildenhall, the USAF bases, were all in the East Anglian region (in 1989), as were many RAF bases: Coltishall, Wittering, Honington and West Rayham.₄ This was also where the SAM defence sites were: at Woodbridge, Wyton, Barkston Heath, etc.

In 1983, America had major military bases in countries such as Egypt, Oman, Japan, Guam, Somalia, Antigua, Ascension Island, Puerto Rico, Greenland and the Philippines. The Soviet Union maintained bases in, among others, Iraq, Yemen, India, Cambodia, Vietnam, Angola, Congo, Mali, Peru, Cuba and Libya. The UK in 1983 had bases in Ghana, Zimbabwe, the Falklands, Hong Kong, Cyprus, Brunei, Ascension and Gibraltar (Sivard, 1982). The American military presence in Britain was massive in the 1970s and 80s. As Radio Moscow put it (in 1984): 'the United Kingdom is literally covered with a dense network of US airforce bases'. For example, at the headquarters of the US 3rd Air Force in Mildenhall, Suffolk, in 1989, there were 16 C-130 Hercules planes, KC-135 Stratotankers, EC-135H airborne C₂ ('command and control') planes, and four SR-71 *Blackbird* aircraft of the 9th Strategic Reconnaissance Wing of Strategic Air Command. There were 4 squadrons of American F-111 long-range bombers in Britain in 1989, as well as 2 squadrons of RAF Tornado Interdiction bombers, 2 squadrons of Buccaneer long-range bombers, 6 squadrons of American A10A Thunderbolt jets, and, with RAF Germany, 7 squadrons of RAF Strike/ Attack Tornado jets. The British government and the Ministry of Defence tried to play down the number of American bases on British soil. Asked about this topic in 1980 the Defence Secretary told the House of Commons there were twelve US bases. A month later he gave 38 names. Asked again a month later, the Defence Secretary admitted to 53 bases. Later in 1980, the MoD acknowledged ten more. In 1983, the MoD said there 75 in total. *The New Statesman* reckoned there were

107 bases in November 1980.

The SR-71 *Blackbird* aircraft, based at the USAF base Mildenhall in Suffolk is intended to fly at 80,000 feet and over 2,000 mph to gather information on the enemy. The intelligence it garners will be available to NATO; however, the US Navy bases (Holy Loch and Thurso in Scotland for example) are primarily to serve US military interests (Dewar, 111). The largest US navy base, at Holy Loch, serves American nuclear-powered ballistic submarines that are visiting or based there. Some of the US bases share intelligence with British forces: the microwave communications link station at Thurso, which uses the LORAN radio navigation system for American nuclear subs is also used by the Royal Navy.[5]

It is worth remembering that, as far as America is concerned, and despite the Anglo-American 'special relationship', Britain is just 'one important ally among several' for the US.[6] During the 1973 Arab-Israeli war, for example, US bases were involved in a global alert but without consulting the UK administration first. What Britain has to do in its defence policy, according to some commentators, is to keep America firmly committed to the defence of Europe, and to Britain in particular. Britain must keep America interested in the defence of Britain, for a number of reasons, not least being the important economic benefits the UK gains from the presence of American forces. With the decision to buy Trident C4 from the Americans, Britain's dependency on the US was further strengthened.

THE GULF WAR

Ironically, in the Gulf War, the US president (George Bush) called upon God (like most US presidents). The phrase 'God bless America' was employed by the US war media machine. But George Bush's invoking of God provoked disbelief in the Arab world, where America was seen as a capitalist, God-less country. People in the Middle East were apparently 'agog' at this appropriation of the deity in the Gulf War (Mernissi, 1992). The Persian Gulf War was the first major test of the vast military space programme of the US (a $200 billion business). It was also the test of the one billion dollar investment that Britain and France had made in space military technology. The hardware and systems employed in the Gulf War by America included LACROSSE satellites for gathering radar pictures; Project White Cloud spacecraft for identifying enemy ships; the Jumpseat satellite for listening in to electronic transmissions; KH-11 satellites for high-quality photos; and Magnum satellites for tapping telephones. (Satellite surveillance is improving all the time: in the future satellites will be able to see each mortar and gun, and right under the seas). Over the desert flew Pioneer RPVs flew (pilotless, remote controlled planes). The Pioneer RPVs flew on 330 sorties, checking for mines, bomb damage, tracking Iraqi mobile missile launchers, and locating Silkworm missiles sites. The data collected in these computer-controlled flights was given to the Av-8B and Cobra aircraft. Other pilotless aircraft robots included the French-manufactured MART, the CL-89 (from Canada), and a Pointer robot (an experimental drone used by the US 82nd Airborne).

The communications operation in the Persian Gulf consisted of a network of 118 mobile satellite ground stations, 12 commercial satellite terminals, which employed 81 switches for 30 message circuits and 329 voice circuits. The battle in the air used nearly 30 million telephone calls. Up to 700,000 telephone calls and 152,000 messages on 30,000 radio frequencies were carried between North America and the Gulf each day.

Despite the emphasis on the new 'smart' technology and the F-117 'stealth' bombers used in the Gulf War, much of the bombing was conventional, Second World War style. That is, dropping stacks of conventional bombs to demoralize (and kill) the enemy. The number of aircraft buzzing around the war zone in the Gulf was tremendous: the 'airspace managers' had to make sense of huge numbers of tasks and orders. Spread over 93,600 miles there were 660 restricted operation zones, 312 missile engagement zones, 78 strike corridors, 932 combat air patrol points, 122 different air refuelling tracks and 36 training areas. On the ground, there were half a million troops, 10,000 tanks and artillery, more than 100,000 jeeps, trucks and vehicles and 1,900 helicopters. The Allied bombing in the Gulf War was largely a failure: 70% of 88,500 tons of bombs missed their targets. Only 6,520 bombs dropped on Iraq and occupied Kuwait were precision-guided.

RUSSIA

Some commentators claim that Russia would accept a huge loss of life in a (nuclear) conflict. It sustained gigantic losses in the Second World War, and might be prepared to do so again (Kahn, 1960, 132). No way would the UK or US accept similar losses (say 5-10 million) or even equivalent losses, in terms of percentage of the total population. It is not certain, either, that massive civilian casualties would accelerate surrender (Ikle, 1958, 192). Commentators cite the Hiroshima and Nagasaki bombs: did these really speed up Japan's surrender? Similarly, the bombing of Dresden killed 30,000 people (or 135,000, depending on which report you consult) but did not instantly lead to the German surrender. An ironic thing is that the more losses increase, the less likely surrender may be. This is the 'level of damage paradox'.

One Oxford professor said (in 1984) that if Britain unilaterally disarmed and Russia invaded Britain, it might not be as bad as imagined at first. Russia at this time might not have wished to add Britain to its problems anyway, and Britain might not be able to prevent a Russian invasion anyway (the West had not prevented Czechoslovakia or Hungary).[7] Though a Russian occupation would be no doubt be grim, it might be better than America's intervention in Chile, or the CIA's regime of the colonels in Greece, or Pol Pot's regime, or South Africa. If Russia or whoever attacked Britain it is likely that it would wish to consolidate its victory and invade, stripping Britain of its capital assets and turning the economy over to Russian advantage. A likely time for invasion is between 9 and 12 months after the attack, when radiation levels are low.

Post-Cold War Russia is seen as particularly worrying for the liberal West. Following the break-up of the old Soviet Union, 2,400 nuclear warheads and 360 ICBMs remained in the new states of Ukraine, Belarus and Kazakhstan. But by the mid-1990s the decommissioning and dismantling process had hardly begun. Further, the state of the missile silos (in Ukraine, for example) were very poor (see Klare, 1993; Cimbala, 1993). Workers at these sites are exposed to twice the acceptable level of radiation. Twenty military sites have had their security systems broken into: no one seems to be absolutely sure what is where, or whether the control codes have been cracked. A nuclear catastrophe was/ is likely, perhaps another Chernobyl was/ is likely. While Belarus ratified START I and the Non-Proliferation Treaty in

February 1993, and Kazakhstan appeared to be following suit, Ukraine was ambiguous about its proposal to become a 'nuclear-free state'. With its 1,600 warheads (of those, 1,240 were ICBMs), Ukraine was 'technically the third most powerful nuclear state of the world' (Erickson, 14). Russia was ringed by armed conflicts in the late 80s/ early 1990s: the former Yugoslavia, Georgia, Azerbaidzhan, Afghanistan and Chechenyia. (Afghanistan was a hot spot way into the 2000s). The image of post-1989 Russia is of a country too vast to control, too old-fashioned in its policies and technology, too unwieldly, too intransigent, too complex, wracked by internal turmoil. The image in the West is of an enormous superpower with a huge nuclear arsenal which's rotting away. Some sites are poorly maintained, while some nuclear hardware is protected by nothing more hefty than a padlock on a railway truck.

Between 1992 and 1996 there were 1,000 reported incidents of nuclear materials being smuggled and sold. Most of these 1,000 claims turned out to be hoaxes, but six of them involved radioactive materials. There may be many more cases other than the six known. In 1994 six lbs of uranium was found on the back seat of a car in Prague. Anyone can find out how to make an atomic bomb: the information is in the public domain. It is the engineering required to construct a bomb that is difficult to obtain. The threat of nuclear terrorism, then, is not as imminent as might be expected, because 'only a fairly large and sophisticated engineering organisation with a great deal of money could replicate' atomic bombs.[8] However, terrorists may already have had nuclear weapons by 1996: in the South Ossetia region of the former Soviet republic of Georgia a political group was rumoured to have had a battlefield nuclear weapon since 1993.

In September 1995 *The Times* reported that Russia was planning to redeploy its forces and to defend itself again against NATO. As NATO was advancing eastwards through Europe, the Russian

Foreign Intelligence Service was monitoring all NATO's military movements in Eastern Europe.[9] China is the third largest or strongest force in the world, with an army (in the mid-1990s) of 3 million (reduced from four million in 1980). China has an airforce comprising 4,500 combat planes, although many of these aircraft are now obsolete, compared to the latest 'smart' technology, which is necessary to win an air battle. China in the 1990s was developing a wide range of nuclear weaponry; nuclear arms were seen by China as essential to obtain the prominence in world politics it desired.[10]

NOTES

1. See Franklin, 1988, 166-7; Kennan, 1983, 177-8
2. Quoted in Franklin, 1988, 199
3. The first use nuclear tactic was denied by the Mother of Parliaments. See General Leopold Chalupa: "The Defence of Central Europe: Implications of Change", *Journal of the Royal United Services Institute for Defence Studies*, March 1985; on US strategy: US Congressional Record. Hearings before the committee on Armed Services, February/ March 1983 and The 600 Ship Navy and the Maritime Strategy (99th Congress) 24 June, 5, 6 & 10 Sept 1985
4. Major operational centres of the RAF (in 1979) were Abingdon, Aldergrove, Binbrook, Brawdy, Brize Norton, Conningsby, Cottesmore, Coleshall, Fairford, Finningley, Kinloss, Leeming, Lossiemouth, Linton-on-Ouse, Lynham, Leuchars, Manston, Machrihanish, Skampton, St Mawgen, Upper Heyford, Waddington and Wittering. (Clarke, 144)
5. Captain Jerry Pape, US Naval Authority, in Duke, 209
6. Christopher Hill: "Reagan and Thatcher: The Sentimental Alliance", *World Outlook*, 1, 2, 1986
7. Michael Dummett: "Nuclear Warfare", in Blake, 1984, 38
8. Tom Wilkie: "Nightmare scenario: terrorists with a nuclear weapon", *The Independent on Sunday*, 21 April 1996, 9
9. Richard Beeston: "Russia 'has a nuclear answer to wider Nato'", *The Times*, 30 Sept 1995
10. Martin Woollacott: "Bargaining with the Bomb', *The Guardian*, 3 February 1996

IV

THE NUCLEAR CLUB

THE NUCLEAR CLUB: BUYERS AND SELLERS

There is (always has been since the origin of atomic warfare) a 'nuclear club' betwixt countries such as Britain, France and the US. The 'nuclear club' is vast and interconnects many nations around the globe. The main sellers and suppliers of technology, hardware and personnel in the nuclear industry, whether civil or military, are Western countries. By 1983, for example, France, Italy, Portugal, Brazil and Russia had supplied nuclear items to Iraq. West Germany had supplied Argentina, Brazil, South Africa and Pakistan. Canada had supplied Pakistan, Argentina, India and Taiwan. France had supplied Japan, Spain, South Africa, Switzerland, Pakistan, Iraq and Iran. The UK had supplied Japan, Pakistan, Spain, America and Switzerland. Russia had supplied Egypt, China, Bulgaria, Cuba, Czechoslovakia, East Germany, West Germany, Hungary, Finland, Libya, Poland and India.

The country that had supplied most countries with nuclear aid and items in 1983 was (no surprise) the US of A: it supplied India, Belgium, France, West Germany, the Netherlands, Sweden, Spain, Switzerland, Mexico, South Africa, Brazil, Yugoslavia,

Japan, Israel, Taiwan, Pakistan, South Korea, the UK, Indonesia, Thailand, South Vietnam, Zaire, Finland, Iran, Philippines and Turkey.

In 1975 the 'London club' was formed, by the seven main sellers of nuclear technology and hardware (the US, the UK, Germany, Japan, France, Russia and Canada). In 1983 there were eight nations that possessed nuclear weapons: the superpowers, France, India, China, UK, South Africa and Israel. Fourteen more nations showed interest in acquiring nuclear weapons: Brazil, Argentina, Mexico, Spain, Iraq, Iran, Egypt, Pakistan, Japan, South Korea, Taiwan, Thailand, South Vietnam and Indonesia. In 1982 two resolutions were presented to the General Assembly of the United Nations, calling for the cease of all further nuclear weapons production; the 2nd resolution was addressed to the two superpowers, asking them to halt nuclear bomb production, deployment, and to ban all nuclear bomb tests. The first UN resolution was passed (122 to 16 votes, with 6 abstentions), the 2nd in 119 votes to 7, with 5 abstentions. No surprise that the nations voting against the resolutions were the UK, US, France, West Germany, Belgium, Netherlands, Italy, Luxembourg, Portugal, Italy, Spain, Canada, New Zealand, Israel, Australia and Turkey. There were (in 1995) some twenty or so nations in the nuclear club, or nearly in it. Around 50 countries could have acquired nuclear weapons at this time. It is ironic that five of the permanent members of the UN Security Council, plus Germany, supply more than 85% of the world's arms trade (Erickson, 1996, 18). When the French resumed testing in the Pacific (in 1995), it was assumed (by the sceptical media and press) that the Ministry of Defence was profiting from data the French scientists gathered from the underground atomic tests. The British government did not come out and condemn the French nuclear tests for many reasons, but one may be that the British share a common interest with the French in testing nuclear weapons. The aim was 'to keep the bomb indefinitely after a Comprehensive Test Ban Treaty has been signed.'[1]

Up until the Treaty Banning Nuclear Weapons Tests in the Atmosphere, Outer Space and Under Water, signed in Moscow on 5 August 1963, 547 tests had been carried out. Between 6 August 1963 and 31 December 1988 there were 1,244 tests. There was one nuclear explosion per week between 1945 and 1979. America detonated 653, the UK 30, Russia 426, France 86, China 25 and India one. Total: 1,221 (Prins, 1983, 253). The total number of tests made between 16 July 1945 and 31 December 1988 was 910 by the USA, 636 by the USSR, 172 by France, 41 by Britain, 31 by China and 1 by India (Poole, 1990, 239). The size of some of the nuclear tests is astonishing. China tested a huge 3-megaton bomb in 1967; it was a U-235 fission-fusion-fission bomb, an air-burst dropped from a Tu-16 bomber. On Christmas Eve 1967 China tested an air-burst thermonuclear bomb of an estimated yield of 20-25 megatons.

In theory, without nuclear bomb testing there an be no nuclear bomb. Outlawing nuclear tests, then, in a Comprehensive Test Ban, *should* outlaw all nuclear bombs. Or at least the production of new bombs. In 1974 the Threshold Test Ban Treaty did not halt the development of new bombs.

NUCLEAR BOMB TESTS

'Stupid French bastards' go nuclear about Brits

An anti-nuclear advertisement produced by a coalition of Green groups in Britain made little impact at home, but provoked fury across the Channel. [...] Shown on French television news, the advertisement brought a reaction fiercer than anything witnessed in France since the announcement that nuclear tests were to resume.

The Observer, 27 August 1995

Just how thorny the nuclear issue can be was manifested in the controversy and debate that surrounded the resuming of the French atomic testing in the Pacific in 1995. French Polynesia was an artificial economy: it became almost entirely dependent on the bomb. Nearly everything was imported. France gave the Polynesian economy nearly £1 billion a year. There were no taxes. All Polynesians were French citizens. The armed forces took up more than a third of the area's jobs. Between 1966, when Charles de Gaulle turned Mururoa and Fangataufa into nuclear testing sites, and 1995, there were 175 French nuclear tests. Forty-one were in the atmosphere. In 1968 two thermonuclear tests detonated from balloons yielded 1.2 megatons and 2.6 megatons, equivalent to about 190 Hiroshimas. The contamination round the Mururoa and Fangataufa atoll was widespread. French atmospheric tests continued until 1974, when international pressure forced them underground. Scientists thought France's Mururoa atomic tests on the Pacific atolls may have caused geological faults, cracking up the islands, with a risk of radiation leaks.[2]

Some people got very upset by the 1995 tests at Mururoa atoll, calling for an economic boycott of France and French products. 60% of French people were apparently against the tests (in opinion polls). Consumers were urged not to buy French wine, for example. Australia and New Zealand warned that Britain's reluctance to

condemn the nuclear tests would further isolate it from the
Commonwealth. Paul Keating, the Australian PM, and his
ministers, found Britain's predictably low-key response disapp-
ointing.[3] A Norwegian 'activist' blew up a Citroen 2CV, the
Sydney Morning Herald carried a front page headline 'WHY ARE
ALL FRENCHMEN STUPID BASTARDS?', and the French company
Dassault lost its chance to bid for a contract to sell forty Alpha-
Jets to Australia. The protest against the tests claimed that
computers could be used to simulate and forecast atomic
explosions, so the real thing wasn't necessary anymore. The
French government, under Jacques Chirac, insisted that the new
bombs were so complex they had to be tested. Greenpeace, as
expected, waded self-righteously into the fray, pitting
themselves against French commandos. A large anti-nuke protest
flotilla of Greenpeace and other ships sailed into the 12-mile
exclusion zone around the South Pacific atolls. The French navy
seized and impounded ships. In Tahiti there were riots, French
government buildings were set on fire, youths threw stones,
smashed office and shop windows, French riot police used tear gas
bombs and stun grenades.[4] Nelson Orta, a Polynesian economist,
said that the Polynesian did not want to go back to fishing and
farming. 'We are traditionally a pacifist people, but look at our
society now. We have violent TV and a bomb that pays people's
salaries. How much tolerance do we have? when does the fuse
light?'[5]

What the sheer intensity and amount of debate surrounding the
resuming of nuclear bomb testing by France demonstrated was the
widespread condemnation of nuclear weapons by many people in
many countries. However, this debate simply took attention
away, as always in the nuclear issue, from the whole of the
nuclear arms industry, which, in the mid-1990s, at the time of the
French tests arguments, was still busy and thriving. Initiatives
such as the INF Treaty (Intermediate Nuclear Forces) and START

(Strategic Arms Reduction Treaty) did not significantly reduce the nuclear threat. The treaties did not stop the arms race: in Britain alone two nuclear submarines were still patrolling the North Sea – two subs always in operation, one in dock. The Army and RAF were equally busy, training, going on manœuvres, keeping fresh for an attack or whatever was asked of them. As Eddy J. Korthals Altes put it:

> The basic fact of our nuclear age is the vulnerability of everybody, everywhere, even in the most powerful nation in the world. No amount of arms spending is going to eliminate this basic reality. On the contrary, there is ample evidence that insecurity increases with the introduction of new and destabilising weapons-systems.[6]

There are, simply, too many nuclear weapons around. This is obvious. There are too many for adequate nuclear deterrence, and too many for attacks and wars. In a 1980s Cold War scenario, about 400 nuclear warheads would be enough to destroy the 200 large cities in each superpower (a 'large' city would mean one with over about 100,000 people). These 400 nuclear warheads attacking 200 cities each in America and Russia would kill about 100,000,000 people and ruin about half of the industrial capability of each superpower. Although 400 nuclear warheads would be sufficient, each superpower in the 1980s deployed 10,000 strategic nuclear warheads. That is, an overkill of 96%.[7] There are far too many nuclear weapons for the policy of deterrence by Mutual Assured Destruction. There are too many nuclear weapons for any other military strategy: AirLand battle, or pre-emptive first strike, or a 'limited nuclear war', or a contained European conflict. It was not certain in the mid-1980s if the Soviets would launch all their weapons at once: there was a feeling that the Soviet Union would need to keep some nuclear weapons to counter a retaliation (second strike) to a first strike.[8] Cities might be saved from a first strike and used as hostages in future negotiations (Kahn, 1960, 82).

The early atomic bombs were relatively small. The 'Trinity' U235 atomic bomb test of the Manhattan Project at Alamogordo in New Mexico on 16 July 1945 yielded 20,000 tons of TNT. The ironically named 'Little Boy' U235 bomb was surprisingly small in size, and yield about 13 kilotons. However, compared to conventional bombing, the Hiroshima bomb was not that effective: 140,000 died as a result of the bomb within four months (or 200,000 after years), compared to 43,000 at Hamburg in a week in 1943, and 83,000 in one sortie by the Curtis Le May US air force in 1945. Oppenheimer's famous words, on seeing the Manhattan Project's first atomic tests at Los Alamos were 'we knew the world could not be the same. A few people laughed, a few people cried. Most were silent.' (in GIovannitti, 197) The Hiroshima bomb severely affected the *hibakusha* (survivors): they were prone to cancers, leukaemia, strabismus, mongolism, liver cirrhosis, hepatitis, tuberculosis and myopia. People were dying from diseases related to the Hiroshima bombing decades after 1945.

The Nevada bomb tests in America directly affected Britain when dust clouds passed over the UK, usually after 5 or 35 days after the detonation. Finding a site far away from centres of population is perhaps the key problem with atomic bomb tests. Wind direction is also a major factor. But, as Teller and Latter put it in 1958: '[u]nfortunately the bombs are too big and the planet is too small.'⁹ One notorious bomb test took place on 1 March 1954 at Bikini atoll. This was the 'Bravo', a lithium deuteride design, the first of the 'Castle' series. It was a staggering 14.8 megatons – over a 1,000 times Hiroshima. While the US Navy destroyer managed to seal their ship, a Japanese trawler, the *Lucky Dragon*, was subjected to fall-out.

Again and again in the nuclear arms debate, we return to history, to recent (20th century) history, to events such as (for, say, Russia), the catastrophic experience of losing twenty million people in the Second World War, through the Berlin blockade and Cold War, to Afghanistan, and the Gulf War. World War II was lucrative for the US arms industry. America produced over 300,000 planes, 100,000 tanks and armoured vehicles, 71,000 ships, 41 million rounds of ammunition, and nearly 6,000,000 machine guns and rifles.

In the 1980s there was, after the troubled replacement of the SS4 and 5 with the SS20 systems in Europe, a series of decisions which seemed heartening: Reykjavik, INF, Gorbachev, weapons cuts and a nuclear-free initiative. It looked good. For Russia, the risk-zones changed from the invasion of the Russian homeland across the European bridgehead, to (after American, Syria, Israel, Libya and the Gulf) the Middle East.

In the nuclear scientific research field there are a wide range of topics relating to nuclear technology, by no means all concerned with the military applications of nuclear technology. From one publisher (Nuclear Technology Publishing of Ashford, UK) we find journals such as *Radiation Protection Dosimetry, Internal Journal of Radioactive Materials Transport*; books such as *Guidebook For the Treatment of Accidental Internal Contamination of Workers, Thermoluminescence Materials* and *A Guide to Radiation and Radioactivity Levels Near High Energy Particle Accelerators;* and proceedings from conferences with titles such as *Chernobyl and the Consequences in Europe, Accidental Urban Contamination, Microdosimetric Counters in Radiation Protection, Radiobiological Consequences of Nuclear Accidents, Test Phantoms and Optimisation in Diagnostic Radiology and Nuclear Medicine, Intakes of Radionuclides: Detection, Assessment and Limitation of Occupational Exposure* and *Nuclear Transport Systems.*

The level of detail and analysis in the surveys of the nuclear power industry is impressive, but the focussing on atomic radiation and contamination is disturbing as well as reassuring, and is a reminder of the doubts surrounding the nuclear power industry. For example, the Nuclear Technology Publishing's book on Chernobyl states that: 'After the high peaks in the daily air activity concentration of the first week, the main interest has been focussed on contamination of milk, vegetables, food and on *in vivo* incorporation measurements of ^{131}I and ^{103}Ru. Later, the radionuclides ^{134}Cs and ^{137}Cs became the dominant contaminants and will remain so for several years.[10]

THE 'UNTHINKABLE':
RISK, ACCIDENT AND NUCLEAR WAR

Nuclear war is such an overwhelmingly horrific occurrence many (most/ nearly all?) people block it from their minds. As with the knowledge of a terminal illness, the horror of a nuclear attack is suppressed. The denial enables people to live – one cannot keep such fears to the forefront all the time. The denial of the horror is part of the belief that *no one would be mad enough to let off a nuclear bomb, would they?* The assumption is that people trust their political leaders: they vote them in to deal with problems and decisions that require people tackling them full time, as a profession; they trust the leaders to be commonsensical, caring, knowledgeable, morally good. The idea that nuclear war could occur by accident is perhaps even more horrifying than a planned military conflict, which would have (probably) been developing over weeks beforehand, with the requisite whitewash of patriotic propaganda. An accidental nuclear war, though, what a cosmic cock-up. These fears have been explored in films such as the 1983 *War Games*, where a master computer goes mad, like

HAL in *2,001*. An accidental nuclear conflict would doubly confirm the idiocy of nuclear arms. An accidental nuclear strike or war would mean devastation on a larger scale than the Holocaust in WW II, but without any side 'meaning' to do it. It would mean genocide on a much larger scale than the Holocaust or Hiroshima but without the Nazis or the Americans deliberately planning it and carrying it out.

Nuclear deterrence relies upon a number of confusions and ambiguities. For example, nuclear deterrence means that 1000s of atomic weapons must be deployed around the world and must be ready to be launched with a few minutes. A few minutes, not next week, or next Spring, but *a few minutes.* In the two World Wars, military technology was being developed at a furious rate, and the manufacturers had to work like crazy to keep up with the demand of the war effort. Weapons systems took months to be delivered. In a nuclear war, the weapons must be able to be fired within minutes. Yet, the military and governments assure the voters that these nuclear technologies are quite different from all other technological systems, and are therefore not prone to systems failures, mistakes, accidents, wrong or rushed decisions or terrorism. Nuclear weapons are safe! This is the ambiguity of the nuclear arms race. 747 jumbo jets may be sabotaged (Lockerbie), airliners may catch fire on take off (Manchester), roll-on-roll-off passenger ferries may sink (Zebruggee), boats may sink at night when a party's in progress (on the Thames), but nuclear weapons, far more sophisticated and complex than civil transport, will not fail or go off by accident. The nuclear arms debate is full of such impossible-to-reconcile notions.[11]

No one knows just how people will respond to a nuclear war: no one knows exactly how such widespread devastation will affect the decision-makers. In such extreme circumstances, with the life of millions of people at stake in a matter of a few minutes, no one knows how the politicians or generals will react. The number of mistakes and accidents that have occurred in so-called 'peace time' demonstrate that weapons of mass destruction are not 'safe', but in a war situation, they must become far less 'safe'. So many accidents and near-catastrophies have occurred, though, over the years (see Smoker, 1988), that it's also impossible not to be deeply sceptical about the 'safety' and 'deterrence' functions of nuclear arms. Only the total elimination of a nuclear weapon will render it 'safe': while it still exists, in some form or other, it remains potentially harmful.

The total of nuclear fuck-ups, from 1945-1989, was about 1,200. This number, though, is of those incidents that have become known: the real total must be much larger. Nuclear arms accidents are called 'broken arrows' by the Pentagon: there have been at least one broken arrow per year since 1945. In 1975 a fire on board the USS *Belknap* burned to within forty feet of the vessel's nuclear arms. An accidental nuclear war nearly occurred on 8-9 November 1983, according to the spy Oleg Gordievski, when the US military exercise Able Archer was interpreted as a pre-emptive nuclear strike by the Soviet political command.[12]

Major computer malfunctions are not just the stuff of fictional films such as *2,001* and *War Games*. The central computer of NORAD in Cheyenne Mountain, Colorado, told the American defense command on 9 November 1979 that Soviet missiles were on their way. Before it was discovered that a 'war game' tape had been loaded into the computer jet fighters were scrambled. The NORAD computer again told the defense machine (on 3 June 1980) that America was being attacked by Soviet missiles. Nuclear submarines were warned, over 100 bombers were put on full alert by SAC HQ in Omaha, an airborne command post jet took off from Hawaii, and ICBM crews were told to prepare for ignition. It turned out that a micro chip costing 46¢ had shorted out. False alarms are apparently normal for the US defence system. There were 147 serious false alarms and 3,703 'routine' alarms (nearly 7 per day) between January 1979 and June 1980. In the first half of 1980 the number of conferences for 'routine' alarms was 12 a day. Every 2.6 days serious conferences were convened to evaluate what appeared to be missile attacks on the US.[13]

Further nuclear-related accidents include: a B-36 bomber dropped an atomic bomb near Kirtland Air Force base (1956); a B-47 crashed into a nuclear store of three Mark 6 atomic bombs at Lakenheath in Suffolk (27 July 1956), each bomb had 8,000 pounds of TNT; a B-47 bomber mid-air collision near Hunter Air Force Base in Georgia let go a nuclear bomb (1958); a fire at McGuire Air Force Base in New Jersey caused two explosions (8 June 1960); Thor ICBM failure: two 20-24 megaton bombs fell out of a B-52 over Goldsboro in North Carolina: one broke up on impact, the other parachuted to the ground, but five out of its six safety mechanisms failed (1961); 1 megaton was destroyed over Johnston Island Pacific Test Range (4 June 1962); *Thresher* submarine lost in the Atlantic (1963); mid-air collision of a B-52 bomber (with 4 H-bombs, approx. 20-25 megatons) and a KC-135 tanker in Palomares, Spain (17 January 1966); 4 H-bombs lost in a B-52 crash near North Star, Thule in Greenland (21 January 1968); a Russian G-class submarine sank in the Pacific after an explosion (1968); an N-class sub sank in the Atlantic (1970); a *Kashin*-class destroyer sank in the Black Sea (1974); a 20-kiloton bomb container fell down a test shaft in Nevada (1975); a Russian nuclear submarine hit an American frigate in the Ionian Sea (1976); fire at Titan II missile silo in Kansas (1978); false alert at NORAD in Colorado (1979); Titan II rocket explosion at Arkansas (1980); a merchant ship hit a nuclear warship at Malta; in November 1981 a notorious incident occurred at Holy Loch in Scotland, when a Poseidon missile fell about fifteen feet when it was being winched between a nuclear sub and the submarine tender USS *Holland*. Although an atomic explosion did not and perhaps could not have happened, the chemical explosive charge used to trigger the bombs (LX-09) is extremely sensitive (it killed two people in Amarillo, Texas, at the Pantex plant in 1977).

What is the 'risk' of popping your clogs in a nuclear war? How likely is a nuclear attack or accident? Statistics on the probability of dying by causes such as air crashes and murder find their way into everyday life from time to time, as people say, *well, it couldn't happen to me, could it?*

Be careful

…your chances of… dying suddenly, or, to be more precise, suffering a sudden incident that will lead directly to your death. Murder: 100,000 to one (at the hands of a serial killer: 2.5 million to one); struck by lightning: 10 million to one; accident at work: 43,500 to one; accident at home: 26,000 to one; in an air crash: one million to one; in a car crash: 8,000 to one; in a railway accident: 500,000 to one.[14]

People in the UK are definitely not at all prepared for a nuclear (or even 'conventional' major) conflict. Many believe that nothing can be done anyway. Only a tiny minority believe that they are well prepared for an attack. Understandably, a 1982 Gallup poll showed that 72% of adults were worried about nuclear war, and 38% thought it would occur (Ehrlich, 177). Many people (half of the people in London in one 1986 survey) believed that Britain would not be attacked in the next 5 years, and a quarter were sure it would not be attacked in 20 years. People, it seems, genuinely believe that *it won't happen to me*. This happens with cancer, AIDS, airplane crashes, bankruptcy, and nuclear war. *It couldn't be me.* It is a self-delusion that enables so-called 'everyday life' to be endured.

When there is a scenario of warnings and threats, many people do nothing (or next to nothing). They'll boycott French wine during nuclear testing in the Pacific, because that's easy to do: you just reach down an Italian or Australian wine bottle from the racks in the supermarket instead. Dealing full-on with the prospect of nuclear war, though, is something else. The preferred response is 'crisis response' or 'disaster response'. That is, *I'll deal with it when it happens*, or *I'll do something when it reaches me*. People have inordinate faith in protective measures, such as earthquake building codes or nuclear failsafe devices, or the ability of the person in the oncoming car to drive on their side of the road. With regard to nuclear war, the assumption that, for example, the media will tell the public well in advance of an imminent conflict, may be shaky; even an intense publicity campaign, though, might not be enough to convince people of the dangers.

When a flood or a tornado is imminent, for instance, many people (up to 40% in a Michigan 1982 tornado) ignore the broadcast and police warnings.[15] The tornado, or flood, or war, is on its way, and half the population simply goes about its business, or drives nearer to the site, to get a look. In earthquake zones, many people deny that anything hurtful can happen to them. Even though many people have been in earthquakes before, and are sure another earthquake will occur, they still do relatively nothing about it, and are convinced they won't be damaged. Warnings must be expected and clear, otherwise 'people would rather believe they are safe than in danger'.[16]

In threatening situations (such as at Three Mile Island) people have to be told again and again about the dangers. At Three Mile Island factors that contributed to people evacuating the area included the disruption of telephone service and the distance from the nuclear plant.[17] The people who decide to evacuate are often young families, or younger middle class families. The evacuees from Three Mile Island were younger (only 13.8% of the over 60s went, but 46.8% of the people in their 20s). Decisions to evacuate (at Three Mile Island) were often made in groups, particularly the family group. Single people tended to stay put, regardless of their age. If the neighbours left, then they left. In a war scare, the mass media would influence people: men would be more likely to stay put and monitor the media to gauge the seriousness of the situation. Women (especially those with young children) would be more inclined to opt for leaving.[18] Men would prefer to see the visual signs of danger: without visual/ material evidence, people would be less inclined to believe in (and act on) the threat. In an international nuclear crisis, as many as 10 per cent of people would try to carry on as if nothing were happening.

NOTES

1. Editorial, *The Guardian*, 21 Sept 1995

2. Sarah Helm: "Brussels takes on French over nuclear test safety", *The Independent*, 8 October 1995

3. Robert Milliken: "Pacific fury at UK silence", *The Independent on Sunday*, 8 October 1995, 13

4. Adam Sage: "'Stupid French bastards' go nuclear about Brits", *The Observer*, 27 August 1995; Robert Milliken: "Greenpeace flotilla is warned off by France", Tom Wilke: "Paris strives to stay in race", *The Independent*, 6 September 1995, 9; Robert Milliken: "Tahiti in shock after 12 hours ablaze", *The Independent*, 8 September 1995, 12

5. Robert Milliken: "Nuke tests crack colonial grip", *The Independent on Sunday*, 3 September 1995, 13

6. Korthals Altes: "A Diplomatic Conversion: From MAD To Mutual Assured Security", in Barnet, 120

7. Even after the START Treaty, each superpower in the 1980s would still have 6,000 nuclear warhead each, and would still have over 90% overkill.

8. Lawrence Freedman: *GLAWARS Task 1: The Military Threat*, South Bank Polytechnic 1986. For years the Russian military strategy was "Mass Momentum and Continuous Land Combat".

9. E. Teller & A.L. Latter: *Our Nuclear Future*, 1958, 94

10. On *Chernobyl and the Consequences in Europe*, in Nuclear Technology Publishing's Radiation Protection Publications Catalogue 1995, 21

11. G. Flynn & H. Rattinger, eds: *The Public and Atlantic Defense*, Croom Helm 1985; See Public Agenda Foundation: *Voters' Options on Nuclear Arms Policy*, New York 1984

12. G. Brook-Shepherd: *Storm Birds: Soviet Postwar Defectors*, Weidenfeld & Nicolson 1988

13. See G. Hart & B. Goldwater: "Recent False Alerts from the Nation's Missile Attack Warning System", *Report to the Senate Committee on Armed Services*, US Government Printing Office, Washington DC 1980; A.O. Sulzberger: "Error Alerts U.S. Forces to a False Missile Attack", *New York Times*, 11 Nov 1979; R. Halloran: "Computer Error Falsely Indicates a Soviet Attack", *New York Times*, 6 June 1980; R. Burt: "False Nuclear Alarms Spur Urgent Effort to Find Flaws", *New York Times*, 13 June 1980

14. *The Observer*, 10 April 1994 (quoting *Esquire* magazine, April 1994)

15. T.W. Hodler: "Residents' Preparedness and Response to the Kalamazoo Tornado", *Disasters*, 6, 1, 1982

16. H.B. Williams: "Human Factor in Warning and Response Systems", in George H. Grosser, *et al*: *The Threat of Impending Disaster*, MIT Press, 1964, 92

17. I. Miller: "Dispositional and Situational Variables Related to Evacuation at Three Mile Island"", *Dissertation Abstracts International*, 42, 5-B, 2071, 1981

18. T. Drabek: "Social Processes in Disaster: Family Evacuation", *Social*

Problems, 16, 3, 1969; & J. Stephenson: "Disaster Strikes", *Journal of Applied Social Psychology*, 1, 2, 1971

V

BRITAIN GOES TO NUCLEAR WAR

THE COST OF BRITISH DEFENCE

The UK's defence spending has long been controversial and problematic. Nimrod AEW, the Sting Ray and Tigerfish torpedo system, the Tornado GR1, the LAW 80 anti-tank missile, the EH-101 helicopter, the BATES (Battlefield Artillery Target Engagement System), the TriStar tanker-freighter aircraft, the Eurofighter, the ALARM anti-radar missile and the *Upholder*-class boats are among the arms systems that have been dogged by setbacks, overruns, development problems and political debate. There was a lot to go wrong in the 1980s and 1990s: in 1988, the UK was involved in the production or operation of eighteen different kinds of military equipment, and twenty more were in development.[1]

The British often crow about how good they are at inventing, and mutter about how they don't have the money to exploit the potential of their inventions, so the contracts go abroad. In fact, the British, whether they're the government, the military, the scientists, the manufacturers or the 'general public', are just as incompetent as anyone else on the planet. True, the Harrier jet with its Sidewinder AIM9L missiles were 90% effective against the Argentine air force in the Falklands War, but there have been not a few embarrassing military ventures since the so-called 'peace time' era of post-1945. Prestigious contracts, such as the Ministry of Defence's award of £15 billion for the Eurofighter in August 1996 and the £2 billion contracts for the stand-off missile (CASOM) and the new navy jet (RMPA) in July of the same year,[2] were offset by numerous failures. The torpedo system Spearfish, for instance, made a U-turn in the sea during a test run, and raced back towards its launch point.

The torpedo that thinks it's a boomerang

Over the past 20 years, a variety of hugely expensive British defence systems have turned out to be late in service, over budget, unreliable or just plain unworkable... The troubled systems include:
• The Tigerfish, the Spearfish's predecessor, which was still unreliable after 15 years of development.
• Radar systems for jet fighters and Royal Navy frigates that do not work properly.
• A £270m unmanned spy plane which should have been ready three years ago but is still beset by problems.
• Britain's Airborne Early Warning aircraft system, based on the successful 1960s-vintage Nimrod, which could not distinguish between enemy planes and lorries on the A1. After more than £1 billion had been spent, it was thrown on the scrap-heap. American AWACS aircraft were brought in to replace it.
Spearfish itself, designed to hunt down and destroy nuclear submarines with a complex sonar targeting system, was brought into service only in March last year, seven years behind schedule and £175 million over its £885 million budget. Its problems were not confined to its boomerang effect: Dr McIntosh told MPs, that, at that stage of its trials, it was "performing appallingly".[3]

The failure of the GEC Avionics Nimrod system was particularly costly. It was eventually scrapped in 1986 after proving laughably ineffective. It had cost over one billion pounds, and would have needed a further £500 million to get it operating to the original specifications. The UK government bought the American AWACS instead, at a further cost of 860 million pounds. Up to £4 billion may have been spent on defence in unforeseen cost increases in various systems development programmes and manufacture (Baylis, 1989, 157). GEC also buggered up the Fox-hunter radar system for the RAF Tornado jets. It was supposed to identify up to twenty enemy jets from over 100 miles away, but the radar tracking system was only 60-80% effective, and could be jammed.[4] The Foxhunter system was so late by 1985 that the Tornado jets flew with concrete ballast to simulate the weight of the radar system in the jets' noses.

The torpedo that sank the *Belgrano* in the Falklands War was not, as should have been, GEC/ Marconi Underwater System's Tigerfish torpedo, which wasn't reliable enough, but a WW2 vintage torpedo. The EH-101 helicopter system rose from costing £500 million to over £800 million. Further costs were expected. The LAW 80 anti-tank missile costs rose from £28 million to £60 million; the Rapier anti-aircraft missile system rose by nearly 60%; the BATES artillery targetting system by 140%; the *Upholder*-class of submarines by 72%; the Warrior tracked combat vehicle by 17%; the RAF's TriStar tanker-freighters by 40% (the costs of the second batch went up by 30%; the Skynet military communications satellite by about 27% (these are 1990 prices). One report estimated that costs due to overruns on arms procurement was £1,860,000,000.[5]

Atomic waste grows as submarines rot

Dangerous radioactive waste is piling up secretly in two British ports, as the country's ageing nuclear submarines are retired.[6]

Then there's this report of an ammunitions dump which has been in use for over 50 years. The 300 metre dump was used between 1920 and 1976, and contains more than 1,000,000 tons of ammunition. Between 1945 and 1948, 135,000 tons of munitions were dumped in the sea. 40mm Bofors anti-aircraft shells were left there in 1976.

MoD admits true size of arms dump

Europe's biggest underwater dump for surplus ammunition lies a mere six miles off the Scottish coast, the Ministry of Defence revealed in a letter last week. The munitions dump in the Beaufort's Dyke trench, off Stranraer – which holds more than one million tons of bombs, rockets and shells, including 14,000 tons of rockets with phosgene poison gas warheads, is seven times larger than previously thought.[7]

Even in the centre of London there are nuclear reactors and centres. In Greenwich, for example, housed in the basement of one of Wren's 'masterpiece' buildings, there is a nuclear reactor from the mid-1960s, 'a very potent piece of radioactivity in the middle of a civilian area'. It uses 90% enriched weapons-grade Uranium, which's thirty times more radioactive than the fuel used in commercial reactors. The nuclear reactor at Greenwich (called 'Jason') was used to train engineer officers on nuclear submarines. It will take at least 2 years to dismantle by highly trained staff at a cost of millions.[8]

Military jets seem to be crashing all the time – on manœuvres, and at air shows (bad for PR). In a month and a half in early 1996 eight military planes had crashed, including two Navy Sea Harriers.[9] Twenty three pilots were killed in Harriers in military exercises between the plane's first use in exercises and 1996. In the mid-1990s the British Army became concerned about the unfitness of prospective recruits. Young people, it was claimed, were becoming too fat, too thin, too unhealthy. Inevitably it meant lower standards.[10]

In the mid-1990s a battle was fought between two docks for the contract to refit Britain's nuclear submarines, Devonport and Rosyth. After Devonport had been chosen to work on the four

16,000 ton missile subs, it was found that the 1907-vintage drydocks needed massive upgrading, at an extra cost of £500 million. In choosing Devonport over Rosyth, the UK government had to scrap £120 million of its £387 million redevelopment of the RD57 Trident dock at Rosyth.[11]

In 1980 British defence budget was £9.2 billion; in 1984 it was £15.5 billion; in 1989 it was £19.2 billion.[12] On average Britain was the 3rd-highest proportional spender on defence in NATO. In 1980 it spent 5.2% of GDP on defence, was 2nd in rank on defence spending. The 1981 Nott defence review (*The United Kingdom Defence Programme: The Way Forward*, Cmnd 8288) recommended cutting the numbers of frigates and destroyers from 59 to 50, with 8 held in reserve; and *Invincible*-class ASW warships would be sold off; the older carrier, *Hermes,* would be phased out; nearly all auxiliary ships were to be scrapped. The Falklands crisis, of course, reversed many of these reductions and plans. (For years after this there was no major defence review).

The 1990 *Options For Change* white paper was essentially a defence review: large-scale defence cuts were shelved for the moment as the government remained uncertain about the state of post-Cold War Russia. The 1990 white paper recommended that US forces were still required in Europe; that the ability to operate outside of the UK was increasingly important;[13] NATO's deterrent position could be reassessed; fewer tanks would be needed; the BOAR would be considered).[14] Even so, in the mid-1990s Britain had 'more nuclear weapons on its territory than any other European state apart from Russia'.[15] Although ex-Soviet Union countries such as Ukraine, Belarus and Kazakhstan were committed to returning nuclear weapons following the 1992 Lisbon protocol, and had destroyed some SS-19 missiles, the operation was far from complete year after the end of the Cold War.

The Trident programme has been controversial for a number of reasons, not least for its eventual cost. The specifications of the American/ British Trident are as follows: 3-stage solid-propellant rocket with multi independently-targetted thermo-nuclear warheads, weight: 32,000 lbs, 350-400 CEP accuracy, range: 4,350 miles, payload: 8, 10 or 14 multiple re-entry vehicles, each carrying 50 kiloton yield, plus decoy and penetration aids. Originally, the plan was to replace the four Polaris vessels with their British-made £1 billion Chevaline warheads with the Trident class C4 missiles. This was changed to the Trident II, D5, system after two years. The plan was for the UK to build the boats and warheads, but American missiles would be purchased. The cost for the programme was about £7 billion over 15 years (at 1981 prices); the cost of changing from Trident C4 to D5 was £3 billion (at 1983 prices). In 1988-9 the cost of the British nuclear deterrent (Polaris and Trident) was about 6%of the defence budget and 12% of the total equipment arms spending.[16]

At the time of the maximum investment in Trident, Britain was also set to buy more AWACS, Type 23 frigates, EH-101 helicopters, new main battle tanks, Harrier GR5 and Tornado aircraft, as well as developing the European Fighter Aircraft and a substrategic nuclear system. Trident became the focus of anxieties about defence spending. There were alternatives suggested to the Trident programme. For example, for the cost of Trident, Britain could have bought 500 Tornado jets, or 10,000 tanks, or 5,000 attack helicopters at £2,000,000 a piece, or 100,000 Milan anti-tank missiles, or 100 B-1B American bombers. A force of 50 or so B-1B bombers, accompanied by F-111s and Tornadoes, could severely damage Russian air defences.[17]

Buying Trident meant that Britain would have a front-line strategic nuclear weapon system for a fraction of the cost of developing it independently (McInness, 1986). Buying Trident also meant that Britain was further committed to the United States of America. Britain agreed to have the programme refurbished at

Kings Bay in the US. The Trident programme involved close working relationships between the Joint Working Groups at Aldermaston and Los Alamos and Lawrence Livermore in America.[18]

The amount spent on defence decreased in real terms during the late 1980s and 1990s. The cuts of 1990 ("Options for change") amounted to some £600 million. One critic suggested ways in which defence spending could be reduced: scrap the European Fighter Aircraft, the 4th Trident sub (saving £500 million); the new main battle tank (£600 million); a 3rd of frigates; over 50,000 troops could be demobilized; and half the staff at the Ministry of Defence could go.[19] For some critics, some aspects of military defence are not that costly. Large-scale capital costs do seem high and socially outrageous – the cost of the Trident system, for example. However, the yearly running cost of Polaris in 1983, £126 million, was not that much if it contributed toward world peace. At least, that was how the Thatcher administration saw it.

NUCLEAR POLICY

The British nuclear system is meant to be an 'independent nuclear deterrent'. What does this mean, though? How much is the 'independency' of the British atomic defence reliant on the polices and systems of NATO, or the United States, or on other nuclear nations? The point of the British nuclear deterrent was to 'deter' aggression, as the government kept reminding detractors of the nuclear system: '[l]ike all NATO forces – nuclear and non-nuclear' the government said in a 1981 MoD leaflet, 'the purpose of cruise missiles is to deter aggression.'[20] In 1980 the UK government stated: '[t]he Government of the United Kingdom recognise the supreme importance of preventing nuclear war and, as a Nuclear Weapon State, acknowledge their responsibility to do everything possible to avoid the risk of the outbreak of such a war.'[21] An alternative to this government view is that '[n]uclear weapons are retaliation weapons of mass extermination which indiscriminately slaughter both the just and the unjust, the evil and the good'.[22] The idea of most British governments was that the British nuclear force was the best insurance possible against attack from Russia. No way could the British nuke force destroy even a sizeable part of Russia's nuclear arsenal. The idea, rather, was to be seen to be capable of inflicting harm on cities and industries. The British nuclear deterrent was/ is meant to be a psychological threat, the threat of doing a lot of damage to industry and populations. Britain could have attacked the Soviet Union in the 1980s if it wished, although the Foreign Office claimed that there were no NATO missile systems in Europe which could hit Russia. In fact, a Polaris A-3 missile could fly 500 miles beyond Moscow even it were launched from its Scottish base. If Britain used nuclear weapons on its own, escalation would probably ensue, forcing other nations to go nuclear. In another scenario (the 'trigger' argument), if the UK used nuclear weapons alone, without US backing, the use might trigger an American nuclear reaction. Another scenario ('deception') would be an enemy mistaking a British nuclear attack for an American one: the enemy would hit back at America, which would then enter the war.

You can't 'win' a nuclear war, pundits say. No one knows exactly what'll happen. As Herman Kahn put it succinctly, 'no one has fought and survived more than a comparatively small and one sided nuclear war' (1962, 98). Of the two forms of war, the 'slow war' (wearing the enemy down, the 'siege and/ or attrition' type) and 'quick war', disruption and destruction, a nuclear war can only be of the second, 'quick', kind.[23] The point about nuclear strategy is that the enemy has to believe that a nation has enough military power to ward off any attack. It is not much what a nation has, in terms of hardware and resources, but what the enemy believes it has, and how much the enemy believes it would use the weapons. It's no good having a stack of weaponry if the government of the nation says it probably won't use it in the end. A nuclear nation, like any military nation, has to be seen to be aggressive, or ready to be aggressive, if necessary.

To ask some more simple questions: what if Britain were alienated from the 'international community' weeks before a first strike, so that no other nation aided Britain? What if, as with the Falklands War, Britain was pitted against one other nation, in a dispute that only involved the two countries, and the conflict escalated to nuclear level? Would Britain be helped to fight a nuclear aggressor by other (NATO) nations under *any* conditions? Further, why does Britain pose the threat of nuclear retaliation without providing civilian protection from an enemy attack or retaliation?

Britain needs a nuclear deterrent, it is claimed, to be able to be a major player in world politics. Without nuclear arms, Britain would be relegated to second or lower rank among world powers. Abandoning nuclear weapons would also allow France to become the dominant military force in Europe. To be a part of NATO, too, Britain needs nuclear weapons, along with all the other forces of defence and deterrence, according to those who advocate nuclear military strategy. Commentators have wondered just how capable the British nuclear deterrent is: in 1977 critics reckoned that the British nuclear force could not be used as a first strike against a major power. To disarm a first strike against the UK would require (in 1977, and 20 years later) a nuclear system much larger than Britain had or has. The British nuclear force is too small for anything but a 'last resort' deterrent.[24] For a deterrent to work, one's enemies have to be convinced of the deterrent's power, and of the nation's commitment to use it. There is no certainty, for example, that the enemies of Britain are convinced that Britain would use nuclear weapons. In the Cold War, Britain had to have a nuclear force that could hit Soviet targets in such a way as to dissuade a Soviet first strike. If Britain hit Soviet cities, though, retaliation would be inevitable: used independently, Britain's nuclear force alone was/ is not capable of wiping out the Soviet retaliatory force. Without NATO (and the US in particular), Britain (nor France) could not deter Russia on its own.

For much of the postwar era, the British nuclear deterrent was seen as part of NATO: the targets of the British *Polaris* force, for example, were set by an inter-allied group at NATO's Omaha, Nebraska strategic headquarters. Britain was part of the SACEUR network (Supreme Allied Commander Europe). The foundations of the British nuclear defence policy were formed in the aftermath of the Second World War. This is to state the obvious, but so much of the current military and political situation can be explained by going back to WW 2. Even at the superficial and visual level, the military looks much the same as it did in Word War II. Army camps, for example, with their khaki-clad squaddies lurching around assault courses brandishing rifles, and their rumbling green tanks which pound hell out of the Dorset hills, and their trucks and Land Rovers with the canvas flapping as they rattle down country lanes, is essentially the same. Visit an army camp and you could be back in 1943. You don't have to change much to make a military base look Second World Warish (as filmmakers have found over the years). The British government has kept pretty much to the nuclear policies that were born in the years immediately after the war. Take this government statement from April 1957 (Cmnd 124), it doesn't differ much from today's post-Cold War world:

> The free world is today mainly dependent for its protection upon the nuclear capability of the United States. While Britain cannot by comparison make more than a modest contribution, there is a wide measure of agreement that she must possess an appreciable element of nuclear deterrent power of her own. British atomic bombs are already in steady production and the Royal Air Force holds a substantial number of them.[25]

Sceptics of the British 'independent' deterrent have been many. The Admiral of the Fleet the Early Mountbatten of Burma said in 1979: 'as a military man I can see no use for any nuclear weapons which would not end in escalation, with consequences that no one can conceive.'[26] It was always assumed that Britain would not use nuclear weapons first – they were for defence, not attack.[27]

Unilateral disarmament presents problems. It might upset the balance of power between nations and 'remove the whole basis of negotiations for arms control and disarmament'.[28] More and more nuclear weapons is no answer, according to A.J.P. Taylor, who argued that unilateral disarmament was a beginning to breaking the 'barren deadlock' of the nuclear arms race (Taylor, 6).

One of the more worrying aspects of the nuclear issue is not only that the prospect of mass destruction exists, and can occur pretty quickly (within a few hours of right *now*), but that people have stopped being appalled by this fact. Since the 1950s, people have lived with the fact that they could die very horribly and at a moment's notice – but not from a lone psychopath, or a speeding truck, or an incurable illness, but from a nuclear death organized by their governments, and paid for by themselves. Death has always been on the menu, and humans have always lived with it. Nuclear destruction is different, however, from localized conflicts: it affects everybody on the planet.

Possessing nuclear weapons must mean that you might someday in some circumstances use them. Otherwise why have them? Or is it that nations agree to use nuclear weapons if provoked, even though they would not accept their actual use? You must 'show' other countries you are serious about having (let alone using) nuclear weapons. Therefore, to be credible, you must have the latest and best weapons. But the more you develop and manufacture nuclear weapons, the more you are inclined to believe that you can win a nuclear conflict ('we've got the best technology, so we must win'). Also, the more that nations believe they can win a conflict, the more likely they are to use them.

You can't 'de-invent' nuclear weapons, just as you can't 'de-invent' the self-lighting gas cooker, or the cel phone, or the internet, or the i-Pod, or the fax machine, or the car. Once people have got these machines, they would not readily give them up. Few people go back to hand-washing clothes after having an electric washing machine. It's the same with nuclear arms. Even if all nations agreed to get rid of nuclear weapons, and each could see that everyone else had definitely given them up (itself a difficult task to effect), when a conflict arose there is no guarantee that some nations wouldn't quickly rebuild nuclear arsenals. The race to remake nuclear arms would be intense, and would likely lead to pre-emptive moves. Once you've got 'em (nuclear weapons), it seems you can't go back.[29] Just as people get used to the luxury of a washing machine or a cel telephone and couldn't 'manage' without them, so nuclear nations cannot 'manage' their defence without nuclear weapons. Going 'back' to a pre-nuclear world would take years anyway, even if every country agreed to do it (which they haven't, and won't).

Even if all nuclear weapons systems were agreed to be abolished next Thursday, it would take years (and billions of $$$) to do it safely and thoroughly. The scale of the dismantling of the British nuclear force alone would be huge, and would require a mass of planning, resources, time and money. In 1964, for example, the British nuclear force consisted of the following components, all of which would have had to be dealt with in a disarmament operation: thermonuclear bomb stockpile (around 300); atomic bomb stockpile around 1,200); plutonium and enriched uranium stocks; Windscale plutonium separation plant; Calder Hall/ Chapelcross plutonium reactors; Capenhurst gaseous diffusion plant; other nuclear reactors; mark 2 Vulcan bombers, other V-bombers and Blue Steel missiles; Canberra, Scimitar and Buccaneer bombers and planes; the TSR-2 bomber project; the Polaris submarine programme; orders for Phantom jets.[30]

There is no way back, it seems. People won't give up their telephones and return to walking miles to speak to someone in all weathers, or rely on a postal system. Similarly, nations won't give up their expensive nuclear arsenals, even though it's obvious that the 'present balance of terror is plainly not a secure way of keeping the peace.'[31]

The START agreements in the mid-1980s, at Camp David, Geneva and Reykjavik, where there was talk by Reagan and Gorbachev of 50% reductions in strategic weapons, were problematic for Thatcher and Britain. Thatcher chided Reagan for dreaming of a nuclear-free world, and reminded him that nuclear deterrence was essential to European stability. In 1989 George Younger said that Britain would consider its contributions to arms control negotiations – 'consider', but not necessarily 'implement'.

For Britain, the bomb was, according to Ernest Bevin, 'its ticket to the top table'.[32] One of the key elements in the history of Britain's nuclear policies was the so-called 'special relationship' with America, in particular between Thatcher and Reagan. The 'special relationship' basically meant that the British government could exert pressure on both America and Russia (Reagan and Gorbachev). The bilateral influence of Britain on America and Russia was preferable, as far as the Iron Lady was concerned, than the multilateralism Gorbachev was pushing for in the late

1980s. The rapport Thatcher had with Reagan meant that Britain became the third key player in global nuclear politics, after the two superpowers. When Bush became president, the 'special relationship' foundered (although it seems to have been further cemented by 9/11, the 'war on terror' and Britain's involvement in both Iraq and Afghanistan).

Some commentators bewail the paucity of press coverage of nuclear issues. Why is nothing, they ask, heard in the press about Britain's dependence on the US for maintenance, repairs, the constraints on the UK's NATO commitments and targetting information? Britain's dependence on America is large, but remains undiscussed.[33]

More thorny questions: how long will nuclear deterrence go on? Will it still be in place in 100 years time? Or a thousand years? Will governments and nations continue to spend vast amount on nuclear (or military) deterrence? Will people be able to keep nuclear systems continually technologically up-to-date and safe? Will they, over a thousand years, resist the urge to use them? What about the United Nations? How much can it 'police' the world's conflicts? Should it have its own armed force, or always rely on countries to make up a force as required? Is it naive to expect too much of the UN? Should it intervene more often? And how?

'PROTECT AND SURVIVE', OR 'STAY PUT', OR, OR, OR...: BRITISH CIVIL DEFENCE

Civil defence can and should be justified upon humanitarian grounds alone. Yet the West, which prides itself upon its civilisation, individual freedom and democratic governments, could be thought extremely negligent in taking the risk of consigning millions of its populations to needless suffering and death through the lack of adequate provisions for their protection.

C. Chant & I. Hogg (1983, 132)

Britain was and is a juicy target: from Russia's (Cold War) point of view, the UK was highly industrialized; has a concentration of communications and transport networks (naval bases, ports, rail, roads, airfields); it's a key seller of arms; has a sophisticated infrastructure geared to NATO, American and national military requirements; has nuclear depots and stockpiles, fuel dumps, pipelines, arms and ammunition depots; has early warning systems (submarine cable terminals, satellite and troposcatter stations, intelligence centres, radio and radio relay stations, dedicated military landlines); and it is in a very favourable position, geographically and militarily.

The civil defence measures in Great Britain would have hardly any effect at all in a nuclear war. Britain is a tiny island with a mass of targets and a lot of people per square mile. (Britain has one of the highest population densities in the world (594 people per square mile); France has 250 / m²; Italy has 484 / m², America has 60 / m² and Sweden has 47 / m²). Even if blast shelters were built for all the people living in London, it would take a few decades to accomplish and cost at last £250 per person (at 1986 prices). To furnish the population with shelters on a mass scale it would cost £10,000 million for ten million people (at 1983 prices).

The Home Office's publications on nuclear civil defence have been seen as laughable by some critics. The advice in *Protect and*

Survive – to build a temporary shelter in some inner room – was
pathetically inadequate.

> Stay at Home. Your own local authority will best be able to help you in
> war… If you move away – unless you have a place of your own to go to
> or intend to stay with relatives – the authority in your new area will not
> help you with accommodation or food or other essentials. If you leave,
> your local authority may need to take your empty house for others to use.
> Stay at home. (*Protect and Survive*, 7)

This advice derives partly from the experience of air raids in
WW 2. Britain has no emergency accommodation or evacuation
plans, no public shelters, just an early warning system. The only
people having protection in the UK will be government officials,
military commanders and welfare agency officials, some of them
housed in the County Emergency Headquarters. The Home
Office's *Domestic Nuclear Shelters* (1981)[34] made a number of
assumptions about 'average' households which do not apply in
reality. The Home Office assumed, for instance, that no fall-out
would penetrate houses which were adequately protected: their
protective advice did not take into consideration that many
houses would be damaged. Most would have broken windows, for
example, through which fall-out would penetrate. In the mid-
1980s, the Home Office was still claiming that the ordinary
British dwelling offered 'worthwhile protection against radioactive fall-out', in some inner 'fall-out room' which would be
prepared beforehand using the information delivered in an
intensive media campaign.[35]

The basic nuclear shelter is a few old doors or bits of wood leant
against a wall. This sort of improvized shelter might offer some
protection against an atomic blast – assuming your building
remains standing. Placing heavy and dense materials around the
shelter is suggested, to absorb radioactive dust. The advice of
getting into the cellar or basement is also useless, because only a
tiny proportion of dwellings have such suitable sites. The British

Medical Association found the Home Office's shelter design poor (1983). More sophisticated nuclear shelters include digging a trench, covering it with doors, on top of which one puts plastic sheeting, to let water run off, then a covering of at least 18 inches of soil. Entrances are shielded with sandbags, and should as long as possible, to protect from fallout. Such a nuclear trench shelter might survive a 7 psi blast, and a 10 megaton bomb if it was between 5 and 7 miles from ground zero. In the more sophisticated nuclear shelters there are decon-tamination areas, blast doors, vents, periscopes and chimneys for stoves. A big problem is staying in the shelter for long periods of time – up to two weeks, for example. Clean water is essential (a minimum of 2 litres per day per person for drinking).

What *can* you do, then, in a nuclear attack? The better civil defence methods stem from preparation. That is, not making do with the pitiful three minute warning, but with years of planning, production and expenditure. For example, some important civil defence measures include: fall-out and blast shelters for the population, political leaders and key industrial workers; relocation schemes for these three groups; industrial hardening and dispersion; measures to ensure good communications; measures to ensure reserves of food, fuel, supplies; and training for staff in the emergency services.

Up until 1983, British civil defence was pathetic, consisting mainly of ensuring government and administration continued after the nuclear exchange. The general public only got a warning, a bit of advice on building a nuclear fall-out shelter, and information on the effects of nuclear weapons. After the Civil Defence Regulations of 1983 local authorities were required to make more thorough civil defence plans. The establishment of the Home Defence Regions and other local centres went part of the way in creating better civil defence systems. Most countries have little or no civil defence. Nearly all European countries are concerned with civil defence. The *per capita* budget in the UK (about £77 million in 1984-5) is about average for other NATO nations, including the US. The Federal Emergency Management Agency in America proposed expensive and extensive evacuation and civil defence schemes, which would cost perhaps $2,000 million a day to carry out. But the ambitious FEMA plans (for example, 259,000,000 shelter spaces) were abandoned in 1985 after widespread opposition and poor funding.[36] In 1956 the UK government was proposing to evacuate twelve million people, though they wouldn't (couldn't?) say exactly where the evacuees were going to be sent.[37] The Russian civil defence contingencies are impressive (though critics doubt the claims the Russian leaders make about them). Between 100 and 120 million out of 272 people would be relocated in the Russian scheme of the mid-1980s.[38] Although Soviet officials urged that the whole population of Russia should be housed in shelters, the actual figures are far less. The CIA reckoned that early 1980s Russia could shelter about 10% of the workforce (that is, about 15 million people in 20,000 blast resistant shelters [in Gouré, 1983]).

The lack of civil defence in Britain is seen by some critics as evidence that Britain would not use its nuclear weapons.

> Apart from anything else the virtual absence of British civil defence precautions is tangible evidence that, whilst producing nuclear weapons, the UK government cannot really envisage the event of their use, which is in strong contrast to the Soviet Union whose accent on civil defence measures since the early 1960s is firm indication that their strategic nuclear weapons *have* been produced for use. (Clarke, 1982, 91)

British civil defence was dramatically reduced in the postwar years. Between 1952 and 1979 it was reduced by two-thirds (from 451,00 manpower in the army in 1952 to 163,000 in 1979). British civil defence in the 1980s consisted of Home Defence Centres administering 11 Home Defence Regions which were divided into two zones. In each zone there were county war HQs, led by the

County Chief Executive. Various groups and committees would supervise the running of each zone (Welfare, Health, Technical, Supply and Administrative Groups). In each county there would be Rest and Feeding Centres, and larger premises which would be Survival Co-ordination Centres. Volunteer groups and organizations such as the Red Cross, RAYNET (4,000 amateur radio operators), and the St John Ambulance Brigade would also work with regional government, the police and military. The UKWMO (UK Warning and Monitoring Organization), consisting of thousands of volunteers from the ROC (Royal Observer Corps) and Home Office personnel, will provide information in nuclear attacks, including the important details about fall-out (dependent upon bomb size, type of explosion, wind speed and direction). The 870 UKWMO fall-out warning points will be manned 24 hours a day in wartime, and will report to 25 Group Controls, which will report to 5 Sector Controls (Western, Midland, Southern, Caledonian and Metropolitan). Instruments such as the 'ground zero indicator' and the 'bomb power indicator' will provide data on nuclear attacks.

Two countries, Sweden and Switzerland, have the most impressive civil defence measures. They have invested in surviving nuclear attacks, instead of investing in military deterrence. Sweden, for example, has 200,000 people trained in civil defence. It has 342 localities with shelters and public shelters in larger towns which can house 100,000 people. It has individual shelter places for five million.[39] If Britain had Swedish-style shelters, the number of deaths would be massively reduced. In four London boroughs in a nuclear attack 783,000 would die without Swedish shelters; with them, 273,000 would die. Switzerland has half a million people trained in civil defence. Expenditure on shelters comprises 70% of the Swiss civil defence budget. The plan is to provide shelters for everyone.

Many people detest the presence of military in their local area, as well as in the UK, in NATO, in the world. The downside of providing many jobs in an area that might otherwise suffer widespread unemployment, is that the military themselves also create many problems. The swagger and arrogance of the military can arouse resentment with locals; noise pollution is a major source of irritance; large tracts of land are out-of-bounds.

Take Dorset, a beautiful part of Britain (the South-West regularly appears at the top of surveys on the quality of life in the UK): there are two major military centres near the coast, West of Weymouth and around Lulworth. Long sections of the coast are out-of-bounds; many roads are unusable for much of the year; neighbours have to put up with the movement of military vehicles; the pounding of the firing ranges can be heard for many miles around. For years there was a large naval presence at Weymouth, which meant helicopters flying noisily up and down the coast. A military force is useless unless it is thoroughly trained, up-to-date, fit for battle, and so on. So in Dorset one sees the army playing at being the army. There are exercises, tests, trial-runs. It is not a 'game', though, for mass military aggression is the most serious game men play. For years people have tried to get the army out of Dorset, but they have been there since the First World War. The RAF are also a continual nuisance.

Over Wales, school children have been frightened by low-flying jets. When they pass over the noise is 'so loud and horrible', the children run to find cover, putting their hands over their ears; classes and exams are disrupted; some children are too frightened to go outside to play. RAF jets are allowed to fly as low as 250 feet, at a top speed of 517 mph. In central Wales, south-west and north-west Britain, they can fly at 100 feet. Pilots fly even lower. A few fly as low as 63 feet. 85,000 low-flying sorties take place each year in Britain. In 1994 there were 5,779 complaints about low-flying aircraft.[40] The number of crashes by

RAF display pilots at air displays also seems alarmingly high. In 1995 a Nimrod crashed into the sea at an air show, killing the seven people on board. The loss of public esteem for the military at such fatal fuck-ups must be considerable.

NOTES

1. *Statement on the Defence Estimates*, Cmnd 344-1, HMSO, 1988, 47
2. Chris Lockwood: "Linking up on defence", *The Times*, 2 September 1996, 41
3. *The Independent on Sunday*, 10 September 1995
4. The Tornado is not invulnerable, despite being a mach 2, variable geometry multi-purpose aircraft, with supersonic missiles capable of hitting targets up to 25 miles away, with a 100 mile range radar system, computer control 'fly-by-wire' systems, ECM to baffle enemy missiles, and sophisticated targetting systems.
5. In *Defence News*, 19 March 1990, 8
6. *The Independent on Sunday*, 23 October 1994, 3
7. C. Bellamy:"MoD admits true size of arms dump", *The Independent*, 20 September 1995
8. 'The government's controversial attempt to sell off Sir Christopher Wren's masterpiece, the Royal Naval College in Greenwich, is likely to be seriously delayed by the presence of a 30-year-old nuclear reactor in its basement.' (Charles Arthur: "Jason casts a cloud over naval college sale", *The Independent*, 22 October 1995)
9. Christopher Bellamy: "Two killed as Harrier explodes in fireball", *The Independent*, 24 February 1996
10. Christopher Bellamy: "'Less robust' generation leaves the Paras short", *The Independent*, 8 October 1995
11. Chris Blackhurst: "'Loser' may yet win naval battle", *The Independent*, 3 September 1995
12. J. Newhouse, 1989
13. The Falklands war provided a major challenge for British forces: to reconquest territory thousands of miles from Britain. The operation was made easier by new military technology: the huge logistic effort required was made easier by computers, while a Vulcan bomber was able to drop 21 1,000-lb bombs on Port Stanley airfield on a 7,8000 mile round trip by flight refuelling.
14. Mark Hoffman: "From conformity to confrontation: Security and arm control in the Thatcher years", in Croft, 1991, 84
15. Christopher Bellamy: "End of Cold War leaves UK as Europe's nuclear store", *The Independent*, 6 January 1996
16. Cmnd 101-II, 10; M. Bittleston: "Cooperation or Competition? Defence Procurement Options for the 1990s", *Adelphi Paper 250*, Brassey's For International Institute for Strategic Studies, , 1990, 38; Paul Laurent: "The Costs of Defence", in Croft, 1991, 97
17. "Time to Rethink", *Flight International*, 126, 15 Dec 1984, 1607
18. Wyn Rees: "The Anglo-American security relationship", in Croft, 1991, 155
19. Paul Laurent: "The Costs of Defence", in Croft, 1991, 103
20. *Cruise Missiles: Some Important Questions and Answers*, Ministry of Defence, Oct 1981
21. *Arms Control and Disarmament*, no. 5, August 1980
22. Christian CND pamphlet no. 1, *Questions and Answers for Christians*

122

on Nuclear Disarmament, 1960, 2-3

23. Paul Kecskemeti's terms (following Hans Delbrück), in *Strategic Surrender*, Stanford University Press 1958

24. Ian Stewart: *The Future of the British Nuclear Deterrent: Technical, Economic and Strategic Issues*, Royal Institute of Internal Affairs, 1977, 5f

25. *Defence: Outline of Future Policy*, Cmnd 124, April 1957, 2-3

26. Mountbatten in Strasbourg, 11 May 1979, in Poole, 1990, 177

27. Brigadier C.N. Barclay said in 1965: 'I think it can be taken as basic to the consideration of this problem that no British government in the foreseeable future could ever be the first to use nuclear weapons.' ("Britain's Independent Deterrent", *Brassey's Annual 1965*, Clowes, 1965, 88

28. Church Assembly Board for Social Responsibility: *Modern War: What Can Christians Do Together?*, Church Information Office 1962

29. J.B. Priestley wrote: 'The only move left than can mean anything is to go into reverse, decisively rejecting nuclear warfare.' (555)

30. Listed in Leonard Beaton: "Would Labour Give Up the Bomb?", *Sunday Telegraph*, August 1964, 11-12

31. *The Church and the Bomb: Nuclear Weapons and Christian Conscience*, [Report of a Working Party under the chairmanship of the Bishop of Salisbury], Hodder & Stoughton 1982, 159

32. Martin Woollacott: "Bargaining with the Bomb', *The Guardian*, 3 February 1996

33. John Eldridge: "Do the Media Promote a Nuclear Mentality?", in Barnett, 66

34. Home Office: *Domestic Nuclear Shelters: Technical Guidance*, HMSO 1981

35. Home Office, *Emergency Planning Guidance to Local Authorities*, Home Office 1985

36. FEMA: *Questions and Answers on Crisis Relocation Planning*, Washington DC, 1980; FEMA: *Civil Defence Program Overview*, Washington DC 1984; Lawrence Vale: *GLAWARS Task 12: Alternative Possible Approaches to Civil Defence*, South Bank Polytechnic 1986

37. Speech by Sir Walter Monckton, House of Commons Debate, *Hansard*, col. 1032-3, 28 Feb 1956

38. L. Gouré: *The Soviet Crisis Relocation Program*, Science Applications, Inc, McLean, Virginia 1983; Gouré: *A Comparison of Soviet and US Civil Defence Programs*, Federal Management Agency, 1983

39. Diane Diacon: *Residential Housing and Nuclear Attack*, Croom Helm 1984; Swedish Civil Defence Administration: *The Swedish Civil Defence*, SCDA, Stockholm 1985

VI

GOD AND THE BOMB

'NO NUKES': ALTERNATIVE MILITARY STRATEGIES

The point about the nuclear issue is that everything is *already in place* for war. It's not as if a massive industrial 'war effort' has to be undertaken, a mass construction of planes, tanks, guns, ships, as in the First and Second World Wars. No need. *They are already in place.* Everything there. Of course, a few subs and planes need to be scrambled and moved to certain locations. Everything else is pretty much ready to go. The 'cold war' is, then, literally a war situation, able to turn 'hot' at the touch of a few switches and a few thousand telecommunications. No wonder, then, that many military establishments around the globe are on a continual 'condition yellow alert', or orange, or red alert.

There are alternatives to having a huge nuclear arsenal, of course. Such vast weaponry has only been around for a tiny portion of human history, fifty, sixty years. Gunpowder, too, has only been around for a relatively short time. Ditto bows and arrows, canons, catapults, and so on. People, though, have been aggressive for eons, it seems. There has always been warfare of one form or

125

another. There are alternatives to nuclear arms, which peace research institutions have explored. The anti-war movement, too, is not confined to the Campaign for Nuclear Disarmament: there were over 30 groups who were opposed to nuclear arms in the early 1980s (such as Scientists against Nuclear Arms, and the Medical Campaign against Nuclear Weapons).

The problem with nuclear arms reduction is that it would require the other nations to inspect the weapons systems of nation. This is hardly likely to happen, because it would allow potential enemies to make a detailed record of everything a nation possessed. One of the major elements of warfare is that you don't let the other side know what you have or, just as important, you have not got, militarily. In a game of bluff you don't show anyone your cards – not if you want to win, that is.

The idea of 'no nukes' is enticing, but few mainstream politicians think it a serious possibility in the near future. Denuclearization for Britain, as far as anti-nuke lobbies are concerned, might include the following demands: jets denuclearized; Trident retired; no American nuclear bases; scientific research institutions to help in the denuclearization process; scaling down to a 'minimum deterrent'; advocating a 'no-first-use' policy; improving conventional defence; proclaiming 'neutrality', and so on. Even if Britain did unilaterally go anti-nuclear (which is unlikely) there is no certainty that other nations would follow suit. Such a move would probably be too destablizing, politically, for Britain, NATO and the West – this is the view among many political commentators. For the West, getting rid of nuclear arms must entail also a disarmament of conventional weapons. Nuclear arms cannot be dissociated from other forms of military defence.

There are many ways of taking non-military or non-violent action and protest (there over 125 kinds of 'non-violent action'). Non-violent action might include marches, picketing, vigils, meetings, leafletting and emigration. 'Non-violent noncooperation' might include strikes, go-slows, boycotts, economic embargoes, and civil disobedience. 'Non-violent intervention' includes sit-ins, fasts, non-violent obstruction and parallel government.[1] There have been many studies of peaceful alternatives to military and nuclear defence.[2] Many of these peace study groups, initiatives and books are meticulously researched and laudable, but few nations seem to take much notice of them.

NUCLEAR MOVIES

Nuclear war movies include *The War Game* (UK, 1965), *Dr Strangelove* (US, 1963, Stanley Kubrick), *The Day After* (US, 1983), *Threads* (GB, 1984, Mick Jackson), *Testament* (US, 1983), *Desert Bloom* (US, 1986), *The Sacrifice* (Sweden, 1986, Andrei Tarkovsky) and *War Games* (1983, US). Post-apocalypse settings in movies include the *Mad Max* and *Terminator* series, and *The Last Battle* (France, 1985, Luc Besson).

Sci-fi scare movies of the 1950s included *Them!* (1954) where huge mutant ants were created by nuclear tests in the American desert. Most American atomic films of the 1950s of course were barely disguised anti-Communist propaganda (*The Atomic City*, 1952, *Invasion USA*, 1952, *Hell and High Water*, 1954, *Strategic Air Command*, 1955, *Bombers B-52*, 1957). Only a few films expressed anti-nuclear or anti-violent views (*The Day the Earth Stood Still*, 1951 and *Five*, 1951). *The Planet of the Apes* series of films of the late 1960s and early 70s featured mutants who worshipped a bomb and chanted 'Glory be to the Holy Bomb and to the Holy Fall-out'.

Peter Watkins' *War Game* was shown privately throughout Britain during the time of its banning. It was a long time (some 25 years) before the BBC eventually broadcast it. The BBC was involved in the censorship of other nuclear programmes. John Pilger's *The Truth Game* on the arms race, for example, was delayed until Max Hastings' *The War About Peace* balanced Pilger's views.[3]

Threads was a worthy BBC docu-drama produced at the height of the arms race and anti-nuke feeling (early/ mid-1980s). It showed an attack on a major city, Sheffield, and looked at how people would cope with it. A young white couple and their parents were the main characters; they were seen trying to make a shelter, graphically undergoing radiation sickness, and dying. The pregnant girlfriend survives, giving birth later to a daughter. Post-holocaust communities were seen trying to cultivate the blasted landscape under skies made dark and smoky by filters. A matter-of-fact voiceover related what was happening at each stage in the film. Eventually, the daughter grows, is raped while a teenager by two youths, and gives birth to a mutant, dead child. *Threads* was a powerful film, in the hard-hitting 'realist' style of British television. After *Threads* was broadcast in 1984, a discussion programme followed on the issues raised by the film. All this was couched in traditional BBC public service broadcasting style. *Threads* attempted to show what would really happen in a nuclear attack. It showed working class shoppers, the people seen on *Coronation Street* and other soaps, bunging tins of food into their baskets and nearly rioting in supermarkets; the police and army trying to organize survivors; mass panic; harrowing images of people trying to cope with something far beyond their means. Filmmaker Ken Russell was not convinced by *Threads'* dour view of post-atomic attack: people would not sadly trudge through a smashed world trying to scratch a living from the Earth, they would start up pop groups. In America, a counterpart to *Threads* was *The Day After*, a TV drama shown in 1983 which had the record number of viewers watching a single programme.

Stanley Kubrick's *Dr Strangelove, or How I Learned to Stop Worrying and Love the Bomb* (1963, GB) is perhaps the best nuclear war film. It was made in Britain and starred Peter Sellers, Slim Pickens, George C. Scott and Sterling Hayden. It hits exactly the right balance between the sober and serious nature of the hi-tech war machine and the utter madness of the arms race and atomic warfare. Kubrick was a meticulous filmmaker, who spent years researching *Dr Strangelove*, reading books and subscribing to *Aviation Week* and the *Bulletin of the Atomic Scientists*. Kubrick's film brilliantly captured the solemnity and idiocy of the arms race in the events at three locations: the Burpelson Air Force Base, which sent up the US Strategic Air Command, its military strategy and personalities; the lone B-52 bomber with its redneck gung-ho Ruskie-hating Major Kong (the two bombs in the bomb bay have 'DEAR JOHN' and 'HI THERE!' scrawled on them, as well as, hilariously, the warning: 'NUCLEAR WARHEAD, HANDLE WITH CARE'); and the wonderful over-the-top Ken Adam-designed War Room with Sellers as the liberal President and the fascist Dr Strangelove. There are many delights in the film. The 'hotline' conversation between the Russian and US leaders (the 'hot line' was created just a year before, during the Cuban missile crisis); General Ripper's obsession with 'precious bodily fluids' which might be contaminated by them Ruskies; Scott as General Turgidson performing amazing contortions with face and body. The dark humour is eroticized in *Dr Strangelove*, as one would expect from a script (co-written) by Terry Southern, who wrote *Candy* and, later, *Blue Movie*. There are references to pornography (Miss Scott is 'Playmate of the Month'); we see Turgidson taking the (telephone) call to war just after he's had sex with Miss Scott; the film opens with the mid-air coition of two jets; Dr Strangelove goes into ecstasy when he describes how life underground would involve slaughtering animals and women 'selected for their sexual characteristics'.

There is much emphasis in *Dr Strangelove* on hardware. Stanley Kubrick has long been fascinated by technology. In *Dr Strangelove* and *2,001* the love of technology reaches new heights of dehumanization. *2,001* showed what might happen if technology, in the form of robots and computers, becomes too powerful, and starts murdering people, as HAL does so coldly. Kubrick's fascination with technology is not an isolated case: it is in fact the norm in military, political and social circles. This is partly why *Dr Strangelove* and *2,001* work so well. Kubrick was simply reflecting what was already there – billions of dollars of it). Kubrick is also fascinated by warfare, aggression and military strategy, as his films show (*Barry Lyndon, Spartacus, 2,001, Paths of Glory, Full Metal Jacket* and *Dr Strangelove*). Films such as *Dr Strangelove, Full Metal Jacket* and *Paths of Glory* are very much concerned with the planning and strategy of war. In *Full Metal Jacket* and *Dr Strangelove* we follow the lead-up to conflict, the how and why certain decisions are made, in what circumstances, with what power relations between people and systems in operation. Kubrick has long been intrigued by military strategy (he is a fan of the game of chess, and planned a film of Napoleon's life for decades). In *Dr Strangelove* Kubrick showed that no matter how complex, sophisticated and 'safe' the military system, no matter how difficult to make a mistake, no matter how many levels of command, control and procedure have to be traversed, mistakes, accidents and misunderstandings will still occur. Perhaps the most graphic example of a major mistake in *Dr Strangelove* is the American army having to storm its own airforce base in order to prevent the war.

The ending of *Dr Strangelove* is bitingly ironic, with its refrains of the WW II Vera Lynn classic 'We'll Meet Again' heard over shots of a series of nuclear explosions. It's an ending that is suitably 'apocalyptic', but the black humour could have backfired. The choice of Vera Lynn, though, is perfect. Not only is it a bland, saccharine tune to have playing over shots of global devastation, but is also one of the key songs of the Second World War, the conflict that gave birth to the Cold War and the arms race.

GOD AND THE BOMB, OR RELIGION AND NUCLEAR WAR

The moral and religious dimension of the nuclear debate is problematic. What is the relation of God to nuclear nations? Did God sanction the use of atomic bombs on Nagasaki and Hiroshima? President Truman blasphemously claimed that God was behind America in its use and possession of atomic arms. Christian thinkers have been unable to reconcile the two things: religion and nuclear weapons. Both deal with ultimates: the creation of a world and the obliteration of all human life. For some commentators, the possession of nuclear arms turns people into gods. They now have the power that divinities such as Krishna or Jehovah have: to destroy whole worlds. Robert Oppenheimer looked to the Orient to provide the tropes for the atomic bomb – the 'light of a thousand suns': 'I remembered the line from the Hindu scripture, the *Bhagavad Gita*... 'Now I am become death, destroyer of worlds'.' (in Giovannitti, 197) This was a general trend in mid-century theology and philosophy – to look to Eastern mysticism. The tendency went hand-in-hand with the Existentialism of Sartre, Camus, Heidegger and Beckett.

If the theoretical aspects of the nuclear debate are muddled, it's much more likely that the practical results will be too. The theory isn't fully worked out, and the confusions over the nuclear issue will probably lead to mistakes. The nuclear deterrent involves bluffs, risks, threats and intentions, all 'abstract' or theoretical considerations. The practicalities of conflict will soon shake up these abstractions. If firing nuclear devices at an enemy and causing them the most horrific suffering is morally wrong or evil, as many commonsensical people would agree, then possessing them may be evil. Forget the 'morality' of nuclear weapons, the imperative, for some commentators, is to get rid of them in the first place, before getting on to notions of 'morality'.[3] Simply to possess nuclear weapons maybe morally wrong. Possessing nuclear arms may mean that nuclear nations are also terrorists.[4] Of course, no one (or few) in Western liberal 'democracies' sees themselves as terrorists. It's always someone else somewhere else who is a terrorist – the 'us and them' argument. Whatever *w e* do cannot be terrorist; only what *others* do is. Nuclear arms draws everyone on the planet together. No one escapes. Like the destruction of the ozone layer, it's everyone's problem.

Another argument against nuclear war strategies is that they are now so complex they make the argument for nuclear deterrence untenable. The idea of deterrence is that each side knows what the other would *really* do in a situation. But the strategies and tactics are now so complex and multi-layered, no side can know what the other will do.

The idea that nuclear weapons have 'kept the peace' is also shaky. What has actually 'deterred' enemies? If Britain will never 'actually' use nuclear weapons, then having them is pointless. Merely possessing them does not necessarily constitute an intention to use them. The deterrent argument is based on bluff, which is not the best way of defending a nation. If *any* use of nuclear weapons is inexcusable, then building and possessing them must be too. Otherwise, it's a (costly) contradiction to stockpile nuclear arms, yet always promise never to use them. No government can advocate the possession of nuclear arms *and* the intention never to use them. The Cold War is thus one of the oddest periods in human history: to have vast stockpiles of very advanced weaponry, which won't be or haven't been used. Perhaps we should accept it – that humans have since time immemorial been violent towards one another. What's scary is how desensitized people are to widespread suffering and violence. Somehow, it's accepted that billions are spent on nuclear and military weapons, and that millions have died in armed conflicts. As President J.F. Kennedy put it in his address to the American University in Washington on 10 June 1963: '[o]ur problems are manmade – therefore they can be solved by man.'[5]

Nuclear deterrence relies on some fundamental assumptions: such as, both sides must think and act logically. If they don't, the enemy's behaviour is impossible to predict. Also, both sides must speak the same language of deterrence and armament. If the enemy has a completely different set of tactics, the stand-off of deterrence can't work. In a real armed nuclear conflict, there would be different ways of thinking, acting, communication and response on each side. Nuclear deterrence only works if all sides think there is a balance between their defence systems. Nuclear deterrence assumes that everyone else is also acting and thinking coolly and rationally. The system is presumed secure because nobody would use nuclear weapons because the results would be catastrophic to their own country. As Roger Ruston observes, this is like saying that no one would commit murder if capital punishment were in place.[6] People still kill even though capital punishment exists. The very fact that these weapons of mass destruction exist, in thousands of launch sites around the planet, makes nuclear war more likely.

For some commentators, nuclear conflicts are not justifiable morally, because non-combatant civilians are killed indis-criminately by nuclear devices (in ib., 49). A nuclear war is not a 'just war', because it kills vast amounts of civilians. A United Nations report reckoned that civilian casualties would outnumber military ones twelve to one. That is, in a limited nuclear war scenario in, say, Germany, between 6 and 7 million civilians would die, compared to 0.4 million military.[6] Nuclear weapons themselves are not 'immoral' – it's what people do with them that may be immoral. Nuclear weapons on their own are just bits of machines and chemicals. It's whether people possess them, or would use them, or make them, that may be immoral. One view of nuclear deterrence is that it isn't that bad because it doesn't affect people's lives that much. They carry on living. The populace is at risk in nuclear deterrence, but the threat is not particularly visible in day-to-day life: it's tucked away in nuclear bunkers, missile silos, the military, government documents and communication systems. You don't *see* nuclear deterrence at work, so it seems to be working. You only see it if you wander into the lesser known parts of the countryside and see military emplacements. Or when you see the occasional army convoy. Nuclear deterrence appears to be working partly because it seems to be unobtrusive. Out of sight, out of mind.

NOTES

1. See Gene Sharp in Roberts, 1967; Prins, 1983
2. Sharp, 19991, 1985; Roberts, 1967; Ferguson, 1982; Prins, 1983; Zuckerman, 1982; Wilson, 1983; Baylis, 1983; Dankbar, 1984; Freedman, 1986; Holsti, 1991; Jones, 1984; Renner, 1993; Roger, 1982; Smoker, 1988; Barnaby 1982
3. John Eldridge: "Do the Media Promote a Nuclear Mentality?", in Barnett, 62
4. Susan Khin Zaw: "Morality and Survival in the Nuclear Age", in Belsey, 1984, 132
5. Kennedy: "Commencement Address at American University in Washington", *Public Papers of the President of the United States, J.F. Kennedy 1963*, Washington, 1964, 462
6. Nigel Blake & Kay Pole, in Blake, 1984, 6
7. Roger Ruston: "Nuclear Deterrence and the Use of the Just War Doctrine", in Blake, 1984, 48
8. United Nations General Assembly: "Comprehensive Study on Nuclear Weapons, Report of the Secretary-General", 12 September 1980, 75

BIBLIOGRAPHY

C. Ahlstrom & K.-A. Nordquist: *Casualties of Conflict*, Uppsala University
 Press, Sweden 1991
Robert C. Aldridge: *First Strike! The Pentagon's Plans for Nuclear War*,
 South End Press, Boston 1983
Yonah Alexander *et al*: *Terrorism*, Global Affairs, Washington D.C. 1991
J. Alpher, ed: *War in the Gulf*, Jaffee Center Study Group, Jerusalem 1992
Alternative Defence Commission, Taylor & Francis 1983
C. Andrew: *Secret Service*, Heinemann 1985
W. Arkin *et al*: *Encyclopedia of the U.S. Military*, Harper & Row, New York
 1990
M.J. Armitage & R.A. Mason: *Air Power in the Nuclear Age*, Macmillan
 1983
L. Arnold: *A Very Special Relationship*, HMSO 1987
Crispin Aubrey, ed: *Nukespeak: The Media and the Bomb*, Comedia 1982
D. Barash: *The Arms Race and Nuclear War*, Wadsworth, Belmont,
 California 1987
E. Barker: *The British Between the Superpowers*, Macmillan 1983
Frank Barnaby & Egbert Boeker: *Defence Without Offence: Non-nuclear
 Defence for Europe*, University of Bradford School of Peace/ Housmans
 1982
Lynn Barnett & Ian Lee, eds: *The Nuclear Mentality: A Psycholosocial
 Analysis of the Arms Race*, Pluto Press 1989
J. Baylis: *Anglo-American Defence Relations 1939-1980*, Macmillan
 1981 / 84
—*British Defence Policy*, Macmillan 1989
—ed: *Alternative Approaches to British Defence Policy*, Macmillan 1983
—&K. Booth: *Britain, NATO and Nuclear Weapons*, Macmillan 1989
C.A. Berkowitz & A. E. Goodman: *Strategic Intelligence*, Princeton
 University Press 1991
Philippa Berry & Andrew Wernick, eds: *Shadow of Spirit: Postmodernism
 and Religion*, Routledge 1992
Nigel Blake & Kay Pole, eds: *Objections to Nuclear Defence: Philosophers on
 Deterrence*, Routledge 1984

139

—eds: *Dangers of Deterrence: Philosophers on Nuclear Strategy*, Routledge 1984

Phil Bolsover: *Civil Defence: The Cruellest Confidence Trick*, CND 1982

Paul Bracken: *The Command Control of Nuclear Forces*, Yale University Press, New Haven 1983

Brian Brivati *et al*, eds: *The Contemporary History Handbook*, Manchester University Press, 1996

Patrick Burke: *The Nuclear Weapons World*, Pinter 1988

B. Burrows & G. Edwards: *The Defence of Western Europe*, Butterworths 1982

Christy Campbell: *War Facts Now*, Fontana 1982

Duncan Campbell: *War Plan UK: The Truth About Civil Defence in Britain*, Paladin 1983

—"War Laws 1, 2 and 3", *New Statesman*, 6, 13, & 20 September 1985

D. Carlton & Carlo Schaerf, eds: *International Terrorism and World Security*, Croom Helm 1975

Christopher Chant & Ian Hogg, eds: *The Nuclear War File*, Ebury Press 1983

M. Chichester & M. Wilkinson: *British Defence Policy*, Brassy's 1987

Stephen J. Cimbala: "Nuclear weapons in the new world order", *Journal of Strategic Studies*, 16, 2, June 1993

I. Clark & N. Wheeler: *The British Origins of Nuclear Strategy 1945-55*, Oxford University Press 1989

Magnus Clarke: *The Nuclear Destruction of Britain*, Croom Helm 1982

Michael Clarke & Marjorie Mowlam, eds: *Debate on Disarmament*, Routledge 1982

Carl von Clausewitz: *On War*, Viking, New York 1988

J.L. Clayton: *Does Defense Beggar Welfare?* National Strategy Information Center, New York 1979

E.A. Cohen & John Gooch: *Military Misfortunes*, Vintage 1991

Sam Cohen: *The Trust About the Neutron Bomb*, Morrow, New York 1983

Carol Cohn: "Sex and Death in the Rational World of Defense Intellectuals", *Signs*, vol. 12, no. 4, 1987

J.M. Collins: *Military Space Forces*, Pergamon-Brassey's, Washington DC 1989

Martinvan Creveld: *Command in War*, Harvard University Press 1985

—*Supplying War*, Harvard University Press 1977

R. Crockatt & S. Smith: *The Cold War Past and Present*, Allen & Unwin 1987

Stuart Croft: *British Security Policy: The Thatcher Years and the End of the Cold War*, HarperCollins 1991

—"Britain and the Nuclear Arms Control Process in the 1990s", *Journal of Arms Control and Disarmament*, 9, 3, 1988

G. Crossley: *British Civil Defence and Nuclear War*, University of Bradford 1983

B.A. Dankbaar: "Alternative defence policies and the peace movement", *Journal of Peace Research*, 21, 2, 1984

A. Deighton, ed: *Britain and the Cold War*, Macmillan 1990

I.D. de Lupos: *The Law of War*, Cambridge University Press 1987

C. de Marenches & D.A. Andelman: *The Fourth World War*, Morrow, New York 1992

Michael Dewar: *Defence of the Nation*, Arms & Armour Press 1989

Diagram Group, ed: *Weapons*, St Martin's, New York 1990
G.M. Dillon: *Defence Policy Making*, Leicester University Press 1988
—*The Falklands, Politics and War*, Macmillan 1988
J.A. Donovan: *U.S. Military Force – 1980*, Center for Defense Information, Washington DC 1980
John Dower: *War Without Mercy*, Pantheon, New York 1986
Simon Duke: *US Defence Bases in the United Kingdom*, Macmillan 1987
Col. T.N. Dupuy: *The Evolution of Weapons and Warfare*, Jane's 1980
—*Numbers, Predictions & War*, Bobbs-Merrill, New York 1979
E.M. Earle, ed: *Makers of Modern Strategy*, Princeton University Press 1973
P. Eddy *et al*: *The Falklands War*, Sphere 1982
Anne Ehrlich *et al*: *London Under Attack: The Report of the Greater London Area War Risk Study Commission*, Blackwell 1986
P.R. Ehrlich *et al*: *The Cold and the Dark: The World After Nuclear War*, Sidgwick & Jackson 1984
S. Elworthy: *How Nuclear Weapons Decisions Are Made*, Macmillan 1986
—*Who Decides? Accountability and Nuclear Weapons Decision-Making in Britain*, Oxford Research Group 1987
John Erickson: "World Security After the Cold War", in Brivati, 1996
L. Fenton, ed: *The Psychology of Nuclear Conflict*, Coventure 1986
John Ferguson: *Disarmament, The Unanswerable Case*, Heinemann 1982
A. Ferrill: *The Origins of War*, Thames & Hudson 1988
R. Fischoff *et al*: *Acceptable Risk*, Cambridge University Press 1984
R. Fletcher: *60 Pounds a Second on Defense*, MacGibbon & Kee 1963
D. Ford: *The Button*, Simon & Schuster, New York 1985
J. D. Frank: "Pre-Nuclear Age Leaders and the Nuclear Arms Race", in I. Fenton 1986
—*Sanity and Survival*, Cresset 1967
H. Bruce Franklin: *War Stars: The Superweapon and the American Imagination*, Oxford University Press 1988
L. Freedman: *Britain and Nuclear Weapons*, Macmillan 1980
—*The Price of Peace*, Macmillan 1986
—*The Evolution of Nuclear Strategy*, Macmillan 1989
D. Fromkin: *A Peace to End All Peace*, Avon, New York 1990
Francis Fukuyama: *The End of History and the Last Man*, Avon, New York 1992
J.K. Galbraith: *How to Control the Military*, Doubleday, New York 1969
T.J. Gander: *Nuclear, Biological and Chemical Warfare*, Ian Allan 1987
Tom Gervasi: *Arsenal of Democracy*, Grove, New York 1977
R. Gilpin: *War and Change in World Politics*, Cambridge University Press 1985
L. Giovannitti & F. Freed: *The Decision to Drop the Bomb*, 1967
D. S. Goldman & W.M. Greenberg: "Preparing for Nuclear War: The Psychological Effects", *American Journal of Psychiatry*, vol. 52, no. 4, 1982
Peter Goodwin: *Nuclear War, the Facts On Our Survival*, Ash & Grant 1981
M. Gowing: *Britain and Atomic Energy*, 2 vols, Macmillan 1964/74
O. Greene *et al*: *Nuclear Winter: The Evidence and the Risks*, Polity Press 1985
D. Greenwood: "The Polaris successor system: At what cost?", *ASIDES*, Aberdeen Centre for Defence Studies, 16, 1980
A.J.R. Groom: *British Thinking About Nuclear Weapons*, Pinter 1974

E.J. Grove: *Vanguard to Trident*, Bodley Head 1987

John Hackett: *The Third World War: The Untold Story*, Bantam, New York 1983

M.H. Halperin: *Contemporary Military Strategy*, Little, Brown, Boston 1967

V.D. Hanson: *The Western Way of War*, Oxford University Press 1989

R. Harris: *Gotcha! The Media, the Government and the Falklands Crisis*, Faber 1983

H. Haste: "Everybody's Scared – But Life Goes On: Coping, Defence and Activism in the Face of the Nuclear Threat", *Journal of Adolescence*, vol. 12, no. 1, 1989

M. Hastings & S. Jenkins: *The Battle for the Falklands*, Michael Joseph 1983

Chaim Herzog: *The Arab-Israeli Wars*, Random House, New York 1982

M. Hoffman, ed: *UK Arms Control Policy in the 1990s*, Manchester University Press 1990

K.J. Holsti: *Peace and War*, Cambridge University Press 1991

Michael Howard: *The Causes of War*, Unwin 1983

—*War in European History*, Oxford University Press 1989

E.P. Hoyt: *Japan's War*, McGraw-Hill, New York 1986

F.C. Ikle: *The Social Impact of Bomb Destruction*, University of Oklahoma Press, Oklahoma 1958

Annette Insdorf: *Indelible Shadows: Film and the Holocaust*, Cambridge University Press 1989

J.T. Johnson & G. Weigel: *Just War and the Gulf War*, Ethics and Public Policy Center, Washington DC 1991

Ellen Jones: *Red Army and Society*, Allen & Unwin 1985

J. Jones: *Stealth Technology*, Aero, Blue Ridge Summit, PA 1989

Lynne Jones, ed: *Keeping the Peace*, Women's Press 1983

S. Jones & H Saunders: *Growing Up in the Nuclear Age*, Bristol & Avon Peace Education Project 1984

Joel Jovel: *Against the State of Nuclear Terror*, Pan 1983

J.A. Joyce: *The War Machine: The Case Against the Arms Race*, Discus, New York 1982

Mark Juergensmeyer: *The New Cold War*, University of California Press, Berkeley, CA 1993

Jerome H. Kahan: *Security in the Nuclear Age*, Brookings Institute, Washington DC 1975

Herman Kahn: *Thinking About the Unthinkable*, Weidenfeld & Nicholson 1962

—*On Thermonuclear War*, Princeton University Press 1960

Fred Kaplan: *The Wizards of Armageddon*, Simon & Schuster, New York 1983

A. Katz: *Life After Nuclear War*, Ballinger, New York 1982

H.S. Katz: *The Warmongers*, Books in Focus, New York 1981

William W. Kaufmann: *A Thoroughly Efficient Navy*, Brookings Institution, Washington DC 1987

Douglas Kellner: *The Persian Gulf TV War*, Westview Press, Boulder, CO 1992

George F. Kennan: *The Nuclear Delusion: Soviet-American Relations in the Atomic Age*, Pantheon, New York 1983

G. Kennedy: *The Military in the Third World*, Duckworth 1974

M.J. Kennedy: *Safely by Sea*, University Press of America, Lanham, MD

1990

Michael Klare: "The new challenges to global security", *Current History*, 92, 57, April 1993

R.H, Kupperman & D.M. Trent: *Terrorism*, Hoover Institution Press, Stanford, CA 1980

D. Langford: *War in 2080*, Morrow, New York 1979

J. Leaning & L. Keyes, eds: *The Counterfeit Ark: Crisis Relocation for Nuclear War*, Ballinger Press, Cambridge, Mass., 1984

Ariel Levite: *Intelligence and Strategic Surprises*, Columbia University Press, New York 1987

H.B. Levine *et al*, eds: *Psychoanalysis and the Nuclear Threat*, Analytic Press, New York 1987

Jack S. Levy: *War in the Modern Great Power System: 1495-1975*, University of Kentucky Press, Lexington 1983

Robert Lifton & Richard Falk: *Indefensible Weapons: The Political and Psychological Case Against Nuclearism*, Basic Books, New York 1982

Ira Lowry: *Post Attack Population of the United States*, Rand Corporation, Santa Monica 1966

E. Luttwark: *The Pentagon and the Art of War*, Simon & Schuster, New York 1984

Kenneth Macksey: *Technology in War: The Impact of Science on Weapon Development and Modern Battle*, Arms & Armour Press, 1986

—& W. Woodhouse: *The Penguin Encyclopedia of Modern Warfare*, Viking, New York 1991

J.R. Macy: *Despair and Personal Power in the Nuclear Age*, New Society, Philadelphia 1983

M. Mandelbaum: *The Nuclear Revolution*, Cambridge University Press 1981

Sue Mansfield: *The Gestalts of War*, Dial Press, New York 1982

M.J. Mazarr: *Missile Defences and Asian-Pacific Security*, Macmillan 1989

C. McInnes: *Trident: The Only Option?*, Brassey's 1986

Scilla McLean, ed: *How Nuclear Weapons Decisions Are Made*, Macmillan 1986

Jeff McMahan: *British Nuclear Weapons: For & Against*, Junction Books 1981

R.E. McMaster, Jr.: *Cycles of War*, Timerbline Trust, Kalispell, MT 1978

W. McNiel: *The Pursuit of Power*, University of Chicago Press 1982

L.D. Melvern *et al*: *Techno-Bandits*, Houghton Mifflin, Boston 1984

Kurt Mendelssohn: *The Secret of Western Domination*, Praeger, New York 1976

Fatima Mernissi: *Islam and Democracy*, Addison-Wesley, Reading, MA 1992

J. Motley: *Beyond the Soviet Threat*, Lexington, MA 1991

John Mueller: *Retreat From Doomsday*, Basic, New York 1991

Neil Numro: *The Quick and the Dead: Electronic Combat and Modern Warfare*, St Martin's, New York 1991

S. Nakdimon: *First Strike*, Summit, New York 1987

Robert Neild: *How to Make Up Your Mind About the Bomb*, Deutsch 1981

K.L. Nelson & C.O. Spencer: *Why War?*, University of California Press 1980

J. Newhouse: *The Nuclear Age*, Michael Joseph 1989

Dan Nimmo: *The Popular Images of Politics*, Prentice-Hall, Englewood Cliffs 1974

K. Ohmae: *The Borderless War*, HarperCollins, New York 1990
N. Oren, ed: *Termination of Wars*, Magnes Press, Jerusalem 1982
Ursula Owen, ed: *Index on Censorship*, Writers & Scholars International,
    1/2, May/June, 1994
K.B. Payne: *Missile Defence in the 21st Century*, Westview Press, CO 1991
S.B. Payne: *The Conduct of War*, Blackwell 1989
P. Peeters: *Can We Avoid a Third World War Around 2010?*, Macmillan
    1979
D. Pepper & A. Jenkins, eds: *The Geography of War*, Blackwell, New York
    1985
A.J. Pierre: *Nuclear Politics*, Oxford University Press 1972
John Poole, ed: *Independence and Interdependence: A Reader on British
    Nuclear Weapons Policy*, Brassey's, 1990
B. Popkess: *Nuclear Survivors Handbook*, Arrow 1980
J.B. Priestley: "Britain and the Nuclear Bomb", *New Statesman*, 2 November
    1957
Peter Pringle & William Arkin: *SIOP: Nuclear War From the Inside*, Sphere
    1983
Gwyn Prins, ed: *Defended to Death*, Penguin 1983
—ed: *The Choice: Nuclear Weapons Versus Security*, Chatto & Windus 1984
Bruce Quarrie: *Special Forces*, Apple 1990
Richard Reisz & Bill Grist: *Space*, Bextree 1994
Michael Renner: *Critical Juncture: The Future of Peacekeeping*, Worldwatch
    Paper, Washington DC 1993
E.E. Rice: *Wars of the Third Kind*, University of California Press 1988
Angela Rinaldi, ed: *Witness to War: Images from the Persian Gulf War*, Los
    Angeles Times 1991
Adam Roberts, ed: *The Strategy of Civilian Defence*, Faber 1967
K. Robins & F. Webster: "Broadcasting Politics: Communications and
    Consumption", *Screen*, 27, 3-4, 1986
B. Rogers & Z. Cervenka: *The Nuclear Axis*, Times Books, New York 1978
Paul Rogers: *Guide to Nuclear Weapons 1982-83*, University of Bradford
    School of Peace 1982
J.L. Romjue: *From Active Defense to Airland Battle*, U.S. Army Training and
    Doctrine Command, 1984
J. Roper, ed: *The Future of British Defence Policy*, Gower 1985
C. Rose: *Campaigns Against Western Defence*, Brassey's/ Macmillan/
    RUSI 1986
R. Ruston: *A Say in the End of the World*, Oxford University Press 1989
P.A.G. Sabin: *The Third World War Scare in Britain*, Macmillan 1986
F. Sallagar: *The Road to Total War*, Van Nostrand Rheinhold, New York
    1969
P. Savigear: *Cold War or Detente in the 1980s*, Wheatsheaf 1987
Jean Seaton & Ben Pinlott, eds: *The Media in British Politics*, Avebury 1987
S.M. Shaker & A.R. Wise: *War Without Men*, vol II, *Future Warfare Series*,
    Pergamon-Brassey's, Washington DC 1988
Gene Sharp: *Civilian-Based Defense*, Princeton University Press 1990
—*The Politics of Nonviolent Action*, Porter-Sargent, Boston 1985
M. Shaw: *Post-Military Society*, Temple University Press, Philadelphia
    1991
J. Simpson: *The Independent Nuclear State*, Macmillan 1983
Ruth Leger Sivard, ed: *World Military and Social Expenditures*, World

Priorities, Leesburg, Virginia 1982
P. Smoker & M. Bradley, eds: *Special Issue on Accidental Nuclear War*, Tampere Peace Research Institute, Finland 1988
S.M. Speiser: *How to End the Nuclear Nightmare*, North River Press, New York 1984
P. Steadman *et al*: *GLAWARS Task 3: Computer predictions of damage and casualties in London*, South Bank Polytechnic 1986
Michael Stephenson & Roger Hearn, eds: *The Nuclear Casebook*, Frederick Muller, 1983
J.G. Stoessinger: *Why Nations Go to War*, St Martin's, New York 1974
B. Strauss & J. Ober: *The Anatomy of Error*, St Martin's, New York 1990
V. Suvorov: *Inside the Soviet Army*, Hamish Hamilton 1982
—*Inside Soviet Military Intelligence*, Berkley, New York 1984
A.J.P. Taylor: *The Exploded Bomb*, Campaign for Nuclear Disarmament 1960
George Thayer: *The War Business*, Discus, New York 1970
E.P. Thompson & Dan Smith, eds: *Protest and Survive*, Penguin 1980
James Thompson, ed: *Psychological Aspects of Nuclear War*, Wiley 1985
Alvin & Heidi Toffler: *War and Anti-War: Survival of the 21st Century*, Warner Books 1994
Jay Tuck: *High-Tech Espionage* Sidgwick & Jackson 1986
Michael Walzer: *Just and Unjust Wars*, basic, New York 1992
John Warden: *The Air Campaign*, Pergamon-Brassey's, Washington DC 1989
R.K. White: *Psychology and the Prevention of Nuclear War*, New York University Press 1986
E.P. Wigner, ed: *Survival and the Bomb*, Indiana University Press, Bloomington 1969
Andrew Wilson: *The Disarmer's Handbook of Military Technology and Organization*, Penguin 1983
Solly Zuckerman: *Nuclear Illusion and Reality*, Collins 1982

145

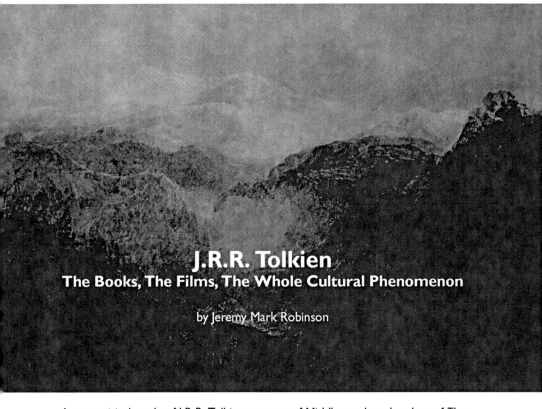

J.R.R. Tolkien
The Books, The Films, The Whole Cultural Phenomenon

by Jeremy Mark Robinson

A new critical study of J.R.R. Tolkien, creator of Middle-earth and author of *The Lord of the Rings, The Hobbit* and *The Silmarillion*, among other books.

This new critical study explores Tolkien's major writings (*The Lord of the Rings, The Hobbit, Beowulf: The Monster and the Critics, The Letters, The Silmarillion* and *The History of Middle-earth* volumes); Tolkien and fairy tales; the mythological, political and religious aspects of Tolkien's Middle-earth; the critics' response to Tolkien's fiction over the decades; the Tolkien industry (merchandizing, toys, role-playing games, posters, Tolkien societies, conferences and the like); Tolkien in visual and fantasy art; the cultural aspects of The Lord of the Rings (from the 1950s to the present); Tolkien's fiction's relationship with other fantasy fiction, such as C.S. Lewis and *Harry Potter*; and the TV, radio and film versions of Tolkien's books, including the 2001-03 Hollywood interpretations of *The Lord of the Rings*.

This new book draws on contemporary cultural theory and analysis and offers a sympathetic and illuminating (and sceptical) account of the Tolkien phenomenon. This book is designed to appeal to the general reader (and viewer) of Tolkien: it is written in a clear, jargon-free and easily-accessible style.

754pp   ISBN 1-86171-057-7   £25.00 / $37.50

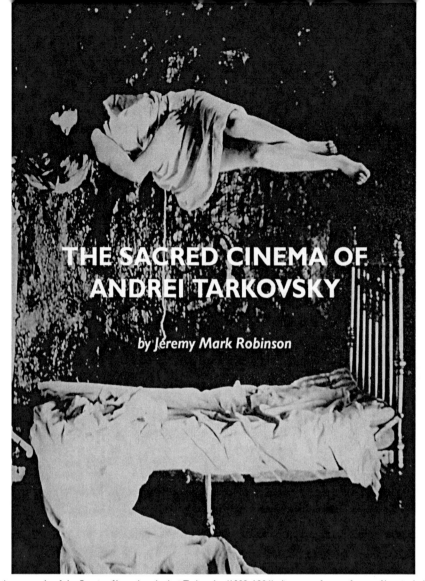

THE SACRED CINEMA OF ANDREI TARKOVSKY

by Jeremy Mark Robinson

A new study of the Russian filmmaker Andrei Tarkovsky (1932-1986), director of seven feature films, including *Andrei Roublyov, Mirror, Solaris, Stalker* and *The Sacrifice*.

This is one of the most comprehensive and detailed studies of Tarkovsky's cinema available. Every film is explored in depth, with scene-by-scene analyses. All aspects of Tarkovsky's output are critiqued, including editing, camera, staging, script, budget, collaborations, production, sound, music, performance and spirituality. Tarkovsky is placed with a European New Wave tradition of filmmaking, alongside directors like Ingmar Bergman, Carl Theodor Dreyer, Pier Paolo Pasolini and Robert Bresson.
An essential addition to film studies.

Illustrations: 150 b/w, 4 colour. 682 pages. First edition. Hardback.

Publisher: Crescent Moon Publishing. Distributor: Gardners Books.

ISBN 1-86171-096-8 (9781861710963) £60.00 / $105.00

The Best of Peter Redgrove's Poetry
The Book of Wonders

by Peter Redgrove, edited and introduced by Jeremy Robinson

Poems of wet shirts and 'wonder-awakening dresses'; honey, wasps and bees; orchards and apples; rivers, seas and tides; storms, rain, weather and clouds; waterworks; labyrinths; amazing perfumes; the Cornish landscape (Penzance, Perranporth, Falmouth, Boscastle, the Lizard and Scilly Isles); the sixth sense and 'extra-sensuous perception'; witchcraft; alchemical vessels and laboratories; yoga; menstruation; mines, minerals and stones; sand dunes; mudbaths; mythology; dreaming; vulvas; and lots of sex magic. This book gathers together poetry (and prose) from every stage of Redgrove's career, and every book. It includes pieces that have only appeared in small presses and magazines, and in uncollected form.

'Peter Redgrove is really an extraordinary poet' (George Szirtes, *Quarto* magazine) 'Peter Redgrove is one of the few significant poets now writing... His 'means' are indeed brilliant and delightful. Technically he is a poet essentially of brilliant and unexpected images...he never disappoints' (Kathleen Raine, *Temenos* magazine).

240pp   ISBN 1-86171-063-1   2nd edition   £19.99 / $29.50

Sex–Magic–Poetry–Cornwall
A Flood of Poems

by Peter Redgrove. Edited with an essay by Jeremy Robinson

A marvellous collection of poems by one of Britain's best but underrated poets, Peter Redgrove. This book brings together some of Redgrove's wildest and most passionate works, creating a 'flood' of poetry. Philip Hobsbaum called Redgrove 'the great poet of our time', while Angela Carter said: 'Redgrove's language can light up a page.' Redgrove ranks alongside Ted Hughes and Sylvia Plath. He is in every way a 'major poet'. Robinson's essay analyzes all of Redgrove's poetic work, including his use of sex magic, natural science, menstruation, psychology, myth, alchemy and feminism.
A new edition, including a new introduction, new preface and new bibliography.

'Robinson's enthusiasm is winning, and his perceptive readings are supported by a very useful bibliography' (*Acumen* magazine)
'*Sex-Magic-Poetry-Cornwall* is a very rich essay... It is like a brightly-lighted box. (Peter Redgrove)
'This is an excellent selection of poetry and an extensive essay on the themes and theories of this unusual poet by Jeremy Robinson' (*Chapman* magazine)

220pp   New, 3rd edition   ISBN 1-86171-070-4   £14.99 / $23.50

THE ART OF
ANDY GOLDSWORTHY

COMPLETE WORKS: SPECIAL EDITION
(PAPERBACK and HARDBACK)

by William Malpas

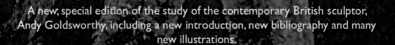

A new, special edition of the study of the contemporary British sculptor, Andy Goldsworthy, including a new introduction, new bibliography and many new illustrations.

This is the most comprehensive, up-to-date, well-researched and in-depth account of Goldsworthy's art available anywhere.

Andy Goldsworthy makes land art. His sculpture is a sensitive, intuitive response to nature, light, time, growth, the seasons and the earth. Goldsworthy's environmental art is becoming ever more popular: 1993's art book *Stone* was a bestseller; the press raved about Goldsworthy taking over a number of London West End art galleries in 1994; during 1995 Goldsworthy designed a set of Royal Mail stamps and had a show at the British Museum. Malpas surveys all of Goldsworthy's art, and analyzes his relation with other land artists such as Robert Smithson, Walter de Maria, Richard Long and David Nash, and his place in the contemporary British art scene.

The Art of Andy Goldsworthy discusses all of Goldsworthy's important and recent exhibitions and books, including the *Sheepfolds* project; the TV documentaries; *Wood* (1996); the New York Holocaust memorial (2003); and Goldsworthy's collaboration on a dance performance.

Illustrations: 70 b/w, 1 colour. 330 pages. New, special, 2nd edition.
Publisher: Crescent Moon Publishing. Distributor: Gardners Books.

ISBN 1-86171-059-3 (9781861710598) (Paperback) £25.00 / $44.00

ISBN 1-86171-080-1 (9781861710802) (Hardback) £60.00 / $105.00

CRESCENT MOON PUBLISHING

ARTS, PAINTING, SCULPTURE

The Art of Andy Goldsworthy: Complete Works(Pbk)
The Art of Andy Goldsworthy: Complete Works (Hbk)
Andy Goldsworthy in Close-Up (Pbk)
Andy Goldsworthy in Close-Up (Hbk)
Land Art: A Complete Guide
Richard Long: The Art of Walking
The Art of Richard Long: Complete Works (Pbk)
The Art of Richard Long: Complete Works (Hbk)
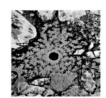
Richard Long in Close-Up
Land Art In the UK
Land Art in Close-Up
Installation Art in Close-Up

Minimal Art and Artists In the 1960s and After
Colourfield Painting
Land Art DVD, TV documentary

Andy Goldsworthy DVD, TV documentary
The Erotic Object: Sexuality in Sculpture From Prehistory to the Present Day
Sex in Art: Pornography and Pleasure in Painting and Sculpture
Postwar Art
Sacred Gardens: The Garden in Myth, Religion and Art
Glorification: Religious Abstraction in Renaissance and 20th Century Art
Early Netherlandish Painting
Leonardo da Vinci
Piero della Francesca

Giovanni Bellini
Fra Angelico: Art and Religion in the Renaissance
Mark Rothko: The Art of Transcendence
Frank Stella: American Abstract Artist
Jasper Johns: Painting By Numbers
Brice Marden

Alison Wilding: The Embrace of Sculpture
Vincent van Gogh: Visionary Landscapes
Eric Gill: Nuptials of God
Constantin Brancusi: Sculpting the Essence of Things
Max Beckmann
Egon Schiele: Sex and Death In Purple Stockings
Delizioso Fotografico Fervore: Works In Process 1
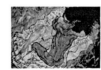
Sacro Cuore: Works In Process 2
The Light Eternal: J.M.W. Turner
The Madonna Glorified: Karen Arthurs

LITERATURE

J.R.R. Tolkien: The Books, The Films, The Whole Cultural Phenomenon
Harry Potter
Sexing Hardy: Thomas Hardy and Feminism
Thomas Hardy's *Tess of the d'Urbervilles*
Thomas Hardy's *Jude the Obscure*
Thomas Hardy: The Tragic Novels
Love and Tragedy: Thomas Hardy
The Poetry of Landscape in Hardy
Wessex Revisited: Thomas Hardy and John Cowper Powys
Wolfgang Iser: Essays
Petrarch, Dante and the Troubadours
Maurice Sendak and the Art of Children's Book Illustration
Andrea Dworkin
Cixous, Irigaray, Kristeva: The *Jouissance* of French Feminism
Julia Kristeva: Art, Love, Melancholy, Philosophy, Semiotics and Psychoanalysis
Hélene Cixous I Love You: The *Jouissance* of Writing
Luce Irigaray: Lips, Kissing, and the Politics of Sexual Difference
Peter Redgrove: Here Comes the Flood
Peter Redgrove: Sex-Magic-Poetry-Cornwall
Lawrence Durrell: Between Love and Death, East and West
Love, Culture & Poetry: Lawrence Durrell
Cavafy: Anatomy of a Soul
German Romantic Poetry: Goethe, Novalis, Heine, Hölderlin, Schlegel, Schiller
Feminism and Shakespeare
Shakespeare: Selected Sonnets
Shakespeare: Love, Poetry & Magic
The Passion of D.H. Lawrence
D.H. Lawrence: Symbolic Landscapes
D.H. Lawrence: Infinite Sensual Violence
Rimbaud: Arthur Rimbaud and the Magic of Poetry
The Ecstasies of John Cowper Powys
Sensualism and Mythology: The Wessex Novels of John Cowper Powys
Amorous Life: John Cowper Powys and the Manifestation of Affectivity (H.W. Fawkner)
Postmodern Powys: New Essays on John Cowper Powys (Joe Boulter)
Rethinking Powys: Critical Essays on John Cowper Powys
Paul Bowles & Bernardo Bertolucci
Rainer Maria Rilke
In the Dim Void: Samuel Beckett
Samuel Beckett Goes into the Silence
André Gide: Fiction and Fervour
Jackie Collins and the Blockbuster Novel
Blinded By Her Light: The Love-Poetry of Robert Graves
The Passion of Colours: Travels In Mediterranean Lands
Poetic Forms
The Dolphin-Boy

POETRY

The Best of Peter Redgrove's Poetry
Peter Redgrove: Here Comes The Flood
Peter Redgrove: Sex-Magic-Poetry-Cornwall

Ursula Le Guin: Walking In Cornwall
Dante: Selections From the Vita Nuova
Petrarch, Dante and the Troubadours

William Shakespeare: Selected Sonnets
Blinded By Her Light: The Love-Poetry of Robert Graves
Emily Dickinson: Selected Poems
Emily Brontë: Poems

Thomas Hardy: Selected Poems
Percy Bysshe Shelley: Poems
John Keats: Selected Poems
D.H. Lawrence: Selected Poems
Edmund Spenser: Poems
John Donne: Poems
Henry Vaughan: Poems

Sir Thomas Wyatt: Poems
Robert Herrick: Selected Poems
Rilke: Space, Essence and Angels in the Poetry of Rainer Maria Rilke
Rainer Maria Rilke: Selected Poems
Friedrich Hölderlin: Selected Poems
Arseny Tarkovsky: Selected Poems

Arthur Rimbaud: Selected Poems
Arthur Rimbaud: A Season in Hell
Arthur Rimbaud and the Magic of Poetry
D.J. Enright: By-Blows
Jeremy Reed: Brigitte's Blue Heart
Jeremy Reed: Claudia Schiffer's Red Shoes
Gorgeous Little Orpheus
Radiance: New Poems

Crescent Moon Book of Nature Poetry
Crescent Moon Book of Love Poetry
Crescent Moon Book of Mystical Poetry
Crescent Moon Book of Elizabethan Love Poetry
Crescent Moon Book of Metaphysical Poetry
Crescent Moon Book of Romantic Poetry
Pagan America: New American Poetry

MEDIA, CINEMA, FEMINISM and CULTURAL STUDIES

J.R.R. Tolkien: The Books, The Films, The Whole Cultural Phenomenon
Harry Potter
Cixous, Irigaray, Kristeva: The *Jouissance* of French Feminism
Julia Kristeva: Art, Love, Melancholy, Philosophy, Semiotics and   Psychoanalysis
Luce Irigaray: Lips, Kissing, and the Politics of Sexual Difference
Hélene Cixous I Love You: The *Jouissance* of Writing
Andrea Dworkin
'Cosmo Woman': The World of Women's Magazines
Women in Pop Music
Discovering the Goddess (Geoffrey Ashe)
The Poetry of Cinema
The Sacred Cinema of Andrei Tarkovsky (Pbk and Hbk)
Paul Bowles & Bernardo Bertolucci
Media Hell: Radio, TV and the Press
An Open Letter to the BBC
Detonation Britain: Nuclear War in the UK
Feminism and Shakespeare
Wild Zones: Pornography, Art and Feminism
Sex in Art: Pornography and Pleasure in Painting and Sculpture
Sexing Hardy: Thomas Hardy and Feminism

In my view *The Light Eternal* is among the very best of all the material I read on Turner. (Douglas Graham, director of the Turner Museum, Denver, Colorado)

The Light Eternal is a model monograph, an exemplary job. The subject matter of the book is beautifully organised and dead on beam. (Lawrence Durrell)

It is amazing for me to see my work treated with such passion and respect. (Andrea Dworkin)

Sex-Magic-Poetry-Cornwall is a very rich essay... It is like a brightly-lighted box. (Peter Redgrove)

CRESCENT MOON PUBLISHING
P.O. Box 393, Maidstone, Kent, ME14 5XU, United Kingdom.
01622-729593 (UK) 01144-1622-729593 (US) 0044-1622-729593 (other territories)
cresmopub@yahoo.co.uk   www.crescentmoon.org.uk

Printed in the United States
146698LV00002B/2/P

9 781861 711731